AN
INVESTOR'S MEMOIR

Don,

To a long time friend
with affection and best
wishes.

Pat

AN
INVESTOR'S MEMOIR

LESSONS LEARNED FROM SIXTY YEARS IN THE STOCK MARKET WITHOUT ONE DAY ON THE SIDELINES!

LEONARD E. GOODALL

Aventine Press

Published by Aventine Press
55 East Emerson St.
Chula Vista CA, 91911
www.aventinepress.com

ISBN: 1-59330-768-3

Library of Congress Control Number: 2012937625
Library of Congress Cataloging-in-Publication Data
An Investor's Memoir/ Leonard E. Goodall
Printed in the United States of America

Table of Contents

Introduction

This book is about my experiences
through sixty years as an investor.

I hope it will also help readers become
more successful investors.

Most of my life has been spent enjoying a very satisfying career in higher education. I have spent my professional life as a professor and administrator, including serving as chief executive officer of two public universities, the University of Michigan-Dearborn and the University of Nevada, Las Vegas. I have been involved with the stock market ever since I was a teenager, even though I have never been a professional or full-time investor.

In August 1952, I was fifteen years old and about to enter my sophomore year of high school. I had somehow become interested in the stock market and decided I wanted to make an investment. Having earned a few hundred dollars at summer jobs, I purchased a small amount (I think it was five shares each) of two stocks, Carrier Corporation and Textron. Carrier later consolidated with United Technologies and ceased to trade as a separate stock. Textron still trades on the NYSE, and I have owned shares of that company without interruption since August 1952. Therefore, there has never been a day in the last sixty years when I was completely "out of the market" or "on the sidelines."

I do not want to imply that I have been an active investor during all that time, watching the market daily, trading regularly, constantly moving in and out of the market, etc. In fact, one of the recurring themes of this book is that the average investor is better off not taking that approach to investing. The individual investor will usually be more successful by investing regularly and cautiously rather than day-trading and trying to beat the market. For most individuals with small or medium sized port-folios, the danger of over-trading is almost always greater than under-trading.

The amount of time I was able to devote to my investments varied greatly from year to year. When working as a university president there were years when I was able to devote very little time to monitoring and managing my portfolio. When I returned to the faculty on a full time basis, I had more time for investing and it gradually became a major research and writing topic for me. I also studied for my Certified Financial Planner designation and developed a small financial planning practice. Most of my early clients were fellow faculty members who came to me because they knew I was familiar with the university retirement system. Even as that practice grew, faculty always constituted an important part of my clientele.

Throughout *An Investor's Memoir*, I have tried to discuss what I have learned and how I have used these lessons in my investing. There are other books where individuals have chroni-cled their experiences over a lifetime of investing, but those I am aware of have been written by full-time financial professionals.

They are people who have devoted all or most of their careers to money management, financial analysis, financial planning or some other aspect of investing. Mine has been very much a part-time experience. Like most investors, I have invested while spending most of my time doing other things.

I have no secret strategies, special systems, complicated charting graphs or sophisticated computer programs to reveal. In fact, a recurring theme throughout this book is that there are no magic formulas or strategies being tightly held by investment gurus, hedge fund managers, Nobel prize-winning economists, computer jockeys or others that are going to make them fabulously wealthy while denying us average investors the same opportunity. Rather, I am convinced after years of watching markets and investors that the most effective investment strategies are also the easiest to understand and the simplest to implement. They have been discussed and written about in a number of books and articles, many of which will be discussed in the pages of this book.

One fundamental lesson I have learned through the years is the futility of trying to predict the direction of the stock market. On the other hand, I have also come to understand that one does not have to predict the market in order to have a successful investment experience. In these pages I have attempted to describe how I believe an investor can achieve long-term investment success without predicting the future, taking excessive risk or discovering any special secrets unknown to others.

This book is not entitled *How to Get Fabulously Wealthy Overnight* or *How I Turned $1000 into $1,000,000 in Just Three Trades.* Indeed, I rebel against such titles. I think they represent much of what is bad about the investment world. People attracted by such books should forget about investing, bring their money to my home town, Las Vegas, and put it in the slot machines. If I have learned anything in sixty years, it is that successful investing is a disciplined, systematic long-term process.

I am solely responsible for the contents of *An Investor's Memoir*, but there are several others who have had a major impact on my knowledge of finance and the preparation of the book. Two good friends, Dr. Bill Corney, a faculty colleague at UNLV and Dr. Bill Stephan, a skilled physician who is also a highly competent financial planner, both made a big difference in my professional life. It is only a slight oversimplification to say that each changed my life with a phone call. In the mid 1980s, Bill Corney called me and said, "Let's start a newsletter." In the early 1990s, Bill Stephan called and said, "Let's start a bank." Bill Corney's call led to the creation of the monthly financial newsletter, *No-Load Portfolios,* that he and I have co-edited for over twenty-seven years. Bill Stephan's call led me to join with him and about ten other residents of Las Vegas to start a new community bank, Commercial Bank of Nevada. Both of these activities consumed a considerable amount of my time in the following years, but both also contributed greatly to my education about the worlds of business and finance.

My daughter, Karen Crane, a professional journalist and educator in Phoenix, has played a crucial role in the preparation of this book. She has read the entire manuscript several times and made both substantive and editorial recommendations. Her professional overview has made it a better publication.

Finally, and most important, my wife Lois, has made invaluable contributions to the book. As with all of my manuscripts throughout many years, she has not only proofread every page, but she has read for substance and suggested changes where she thought they were needed. She often knows what I mean to say better than I do, and helps me say it in an understandable and persuasive way. Even more important, however, she is a wonderful mother and grandmother, and through fifty-three years of marriage she has been the steady hand and moral compass of our family.

Chapter 1
The Early Years

Mine is no "Horatio Alger"—rags to riches—story. I did not start life extremely poor nor did I not ultimately achieve great wealth. I have never been "rich" in the way that term is commonly used. However, my family and I have been able to participate in the gradual but continuing accumulation of financial resources that has come through disciplined, consistent, long-term investing.

I have not discovered any secrets to stock market success. To the contrary, perhaps the most important lesson I have learned over sixty years is that there are no such secrets. Rather, as I said in the introduction, I have learned, as all successful investors learn, that the most effective stock market strategies are also the simplest to learn and the easiest to implement.

Growing Up

I was born and grew up in Warrensburg, Missouri, a small town east of Kansas City. I was fortunate to have wonderful parents and a very stable home life. My father had moved to

Warrensburg from Kansas to be a mechanic in a Ford dealership. My mother moved there from southern Missouri and met my father when he often came to eat in the restaurant where she was a waitress. They married in 1929, just before the depression, and were fortunate to keep their jobs during the depression. In addition, my father used his talents as a wood craftsman to supplement their depression years' income. In his basement workshop, he made wood lamps, small tables and jigsaw puzzles which he sold in the community.

My father's story is much more interesting than mine. A man with an eighth grade education, Leonard B. Goodall was the inventor of the rotary power lawn mower, a subject about which I have written elsewhere ("The Rotary Power Mower and Its Inventor: Leonard B. Goodall," *Missouri Historical Review,* April, 1992). He developed the lawn mower in his basement workshop while keeping his day job. By the late 1930s my father was able to devote all his time to the lawn mower business. He obtained patents and found two local businessmen to support him. They each put in $1000, for which they together received a 49% interest in the business. With their financing, my father formed the Goodall Manufacturing Corporation and spent most of his remaining years manufacturing and selling lawn mowers. My mother left her waitress job and became a secretary in his office.

As the business outgrew his basement workshop, he bought a vacant lot next door to our home, where he built three buildings that housed the mower business. My parents "commuted" to work by walking from our house to the business next door. This meant that I grew up close to my parents. They were home for lunch, nearby when working, and I never suffered from "absentee" parenting. I was convinced I had the world's greatest parents and I have never changed my mind.

For twenty-one years I lived in the same house, from birth until I graduated from Central Missouri State College. After graduation, I left home for graduate school at the University of Missouri. I actually attended all twelve years of elementary and high school in one building. Foster Elementary School was in one wing and the junior-senior high school occupied the rest of the building. Upon graduation from high school, I commuted about five blocks further down the street and attended Central Missouri State College (now the University of Central Missouri). As I recall, the tuition was $92 a quarter, so by living at home and having tuition costs of less than $300 annually, my undergraduate education was amazingly inexpensive.

As my parents' business expanded, they occasionally began buying small amounts of stock. They were never sophisticated investors and, devoting all their time to lawn mowers, they had no time to learn much about investing. I remember my dad saying that whenever he had enough money he would buy ten shares of AT.T., put the stock certificate in his safe deposit box and forget it.

My father was also a great admirer of Henry Ford. He saw him as almost a role model as he built the Ford automobile and created the Ford Motor Co. I expect his years as a Ford dealership mechanic contributed to that loyalty. When the Ford Company announced in the 1950s that it was going public and its shares would trade on the New York Stock Exchange, he immediately put in his order to be on the waiting list to buy shares. I think he was able to buy 200 shares. Years later I inherited the stock and was always reluctant to sell it because I knew how much it meant to him.

As the auto industry fell on hard times, I finally sold the stock in 2007 at a price of about $9. It traded for over $35 in the late 1990s and fell below $2 in the market selloff in September 2008. When I sold, the stock had been in the family about fifty years. This is one of those lessons I have learned over sixty years. Don't fall in love with your stocks, and don't let sentiment drive your investing.

My First Investing

As I discussed briefly in the Introduction, my investing began sixty years ago. In the summer of 1952, after my sophomore year in high school, I saved a few hundred dollars from a part-time summer job and decided to invest it in the stock market. I do not remember why I made that decision. My father invested only infrequently, and we did not have friends or neighbors who were investors. There were no brokerage offices in a small town like ours, and the common way to invest was to go to the local banker who would contact a broker in Kansas City and place the order. He did this as a matter of good customer relations. I am sure he would have preferred that his customers put their money in a savings account or certificate of deposit rather than buying stock. There were two locally owned banks which were quite competitive, so it was not unusual for them to provide their depositors with special services.

I bought two stocks. I think it was five shares each of Carrier Corp. and Textron. Carrier later merged with United Technologies, and no longer trades on the stock exchange. Textron still trades on the NYSE and I have owned a few shares (usually a few hundred) of that company without interruption since August 1952 when I made that first purchase. I have not been "out of the market" since that time.

As the years passed, I purchased a few shares of stock in Textron and other companies whenever I could. As a small investor in the 1950s and 60s, I paid a premium for buying just a few shares. In those days odd lot purchases (purchases of less than 100 shares) carried an extra 1/8, or twelve and one-half cents, on the price of each share. I did not worry much about it because even at that time I was essentially a long-term investor. I did not buy with the intention of selling at a profit in just a few days, weeks or months.

Marriage and College

My early and mid twenties were years in which I had little time or money to devote to investing. It was while attending Central Missouri State that I met the beautiful young lady who would become my wife. Lois was from a small town about thirty miles from where I lived. We were married in 1959, just after she graduated, and we moved to Columbia, Missouri where she obtained a position as an elementary teacher and supported us during the year I was working on my master's degree in political science at the University of Missouri.

While completing my master's work, I was offered graduate fellowships to work on my Ph.D. at the University of Illinois and Washington University in St. Louis. I chose to go to the University of Illinois because I had become familiar with the reputation of Professor Charles M. Kneier at that institution. Beginning in my undergraduate years, I was always undecided as to whether I wanted to major in political science or economics. At the undergraduate level it did not matter. The college was small and it offered only a general degree in social sciences, which included both disciplines. At the master's level I took my degree in political science but audited a graduate seminar in money and banking. At Illinois I was able to combine my interest in the two disciplines. I chose political science as my major field of study and worked under Professor Kneier. Doctoral students had to have a second field of study, and I chose public finance. I had the opportunity to work under John F. Due, who was nationally known for his work on state sales taxes. In addition to being a fine researcher, he was one of the best classroom teachers I had in all my college years.

Professor Kneier, knowing of my interest in the two areas of study, suggested I write my dissertation on a topic that combined both. He suggested I do a study of how state governments attempt to regulate local government debt and the issuance of municipal bonds. It was not exactly an "exciting" topic but it did enable me to pursue my interdisciplinary research interests.

Lois was expecting our first child when we moved to Illinois, so she stayed at home rather than looking for a teaching position. By being careful we were able to live on the university fellowship which I had received and which paid $200 a month. We paid $75 a month for a small upstairs apartment in a private home, and I bought a U.S. savings bond each month for $18.75. We were able to live on the remainder of our income. The two of us were fortunate to have no financial emergencies during the two years we were there, but we had the comfort of knowing our parents would have done their best to help us if needed.

Buying U.S. savings bonds is a practice I continue to the present day, although today I buy them mainly for children and grandchildren. I know all the arguments about whether they are a good investment, and depending on interest rates, they are obviously better at some times than other. I ignore all that debate and buy them because I think they can be a good inclusion in one's foundation investing. They constitute a very small part of my total portfolio, but they are a safe and stable investment and even have tax advantages if spent for education.

Our first of three children, Karla, was born in January 1961, after our move to Illinois the prior August. We have three children. Karen and Greg were born later, and we are fortunate that all have happy marriages and have provided us with nine grandchildren, eight granddaughters and one grandson.

Chapter 2
Going to Work

I was fortunate to finish my Ph.D. work in just two years, so in 1962 at the age of 25, I entered the job market looking for a university teaching position. I had told Professor Kneier that, because of my research interests, I would prefer a position at a state university in or near an urban area and preferably near the state capital. His contacts gave me the opportunity to be considered for several positions. Universities had little money for recruiting in those days, so the practice of bringing potential candidates to campus for an interview, common today, was quite rare at that time. I was interviewed on a phone call from Arizona State University, and I accepted a position in the political science department there when offered. It was exactly what I was looking for. It was near the state's largest urban area, Phoenix, which is also the state capital.

As amazing as it sounds today, when students often graduate with thousands of dollars of debt, I received my doctorate and completed my higher education debt-free. I lived at home as an undergraduate and had very low tuition payments. When working on my master's at the University of Missouri, Lois had an elementary teaching job and I had a teaching assistantship. At the University of Illinois, while working on my doctorate, we were able to live on the income from my university fellowship. We were very fortunate.

A First Job—Moving West

Having been hired by phone and never having been west of the Rocky Mountains, a move to Arizona was a new experience for us. Lois and I, our eighteen month old daughter, and a car without air-conditioning pulling a U-Haul trailer, drove into the Phoenix area in August 1962. We saw a bank thermometer that read 117 degrees and we wondered if we had arrived at the end of the world! As it turned out we quickly came to love the American Southwest, the desert, the sense of openness and newness, the growth and dynamic economy. Years later, when the opportunity came to move to the University of Nevada, Las Vegas, one of the attractions was our good memories of the Southwest from our years in Arizona.

We were at ASU five years where I divided my time between teaching in the political science department and being director of the Bureau of Government Research. The latter position enabled me to direct research projects on a variety of public issues, including a comprehensive study of the Arizona property tax system. That study resulted in action by the legislature that brought major changes in how property taxes were administered and collected at both the state and local levels.

Our second child, Karen, was born while we were in Arizona. She later graduated from high school in Las Vegas, but returned to Arizona to attend ASU where she met her husband. The two are both teachers and proud parents of a daughter and a son.

I had neither much money nor much time for investing in those days. Nevertheless, I did monitor my investments and added to them when I could. Everyone my age remembers where they were when President Kennedy was assassinated, and I remember that I had just left my broker's office in Phoenix. I was driving back toward the ASU campus when the announcement came on the radio.

Although I did not devote a lot of time to investments in my early career years, I did check the prices of my stocks in the newspaper about every day. There was no internet, CNBC, Bloomberg or other electronic way to help monitor one's portfolio at that time. Louis Rukeyser had not even started his famous program on public television. The best one could do to check stock prices was to look at the daily paper which would have the prior day's closing prices. The *Wall Street Journal* was the major source of information for serious investors. Other than that, access to detailed information about the economy and financial matters was hard to find.

There were two times a year when I did devote more time to reviewing my financial holdings. The academic calendar provides certain "down time" for university faculty. One is during summer (if not teaching summer school) and one is between semesters, which usually comes around Christmas and New Year's. Therefore, I had the opportunity to do mid-year and year-end portfolio reviews. Each year just after December 31st, I would sit down with a copy of the *Wall Street Journal* and the *Los Angeles Times*, a yellow pad of paper and a calculator, and go to work. I would calculate the gain or losses for my stocks, their dividend returns, their price/earnings ratios and other pertinent information. It was all done by hand. There was no Excel or other spreadsheet program because there were no computers. I did a similar review in the summer using the June 30th closing prices. I seldom made many changes in my holdings because I was a long-term investor, but I would sometimes "tweak" the portfolio by getting rid of real losers or changing my stock investments slightly. By this time in the mid-1960s my portfolio included my original Textron and small amounts of A.T.T, Pepsico, Colgate and Marriott Hotels. Pepsico and Colgate are still a major part of my stock holdings today. I had begun setting $25 a month aside for stock investing, and while this did not add up quickly, it helped and it was a good discipline for later years when I could increase the amount. I cannot recall the exact dates, but I remember the elation I felt when the portfolio value passed the $12,000 and then the $20,000 levels.

Moving Back to the Midwest

After five years at ASU, I was invited to accept a position in the Department of Political Science at the University of Illinois' new campus in Chicago, then called the University of Illinois at Chicago Circle. It was a hard decision. We loved living in Arizona, and I enjoyed my teaching position. After a lot of thought we decided to make the move. The chance to return to my alma mater, to teach at one of the great, long established state universities and to live closer to aging parents were all factors in the decision.

Lois was pregnant as we arrived in Chicago in 1967. We moved in August, and our third child, Greg, was born in October. We were living in an apartment while our new home was completed. As it turned out the new house and the stork arrived at the same time. We took Lois from the apartment to the hospital, then moved into the house, and when she left the hospital, she and the baby came to our new home.

We were in Chicago four years, and my career changed rather dramatically during that time. It had always been my intention to be a professor, not a university administrator. The campus was young, new and rapidly growing, however, and opportunities for advancement often came rapidly. After two years, I became vice-chancellor, and while I continued to teach one course every semester, my responsibilities became primarily administrative. I enjoyed the work, but it was tremendously intense and time-consuming, and there was little time to devote to investing or anything else.

In 1971, I was offered another attractive opportunity. The University of Michigan was developing a new urban campus in the Detroit metropolitan area just as the University of Illinois had done in the Chicago metropolitan area. They were looking for someone to be the first Chancellor of the new campus. Two good friends of mine on the Chicago faculty wanted to nominate me for the position, and I agreed to have them do so. Because of my experience at two universities and especially my work at a similar campus, I was invited to take the position and became the first Chancellor of the University of Michigan-Dearborn. It was an amazing opportunity. I became Chancellor at the age of 34, and I realized from the beginning how much I had to learn.

An Investment Lesson

The move from Chicago to Dearborn did cause one major investment decision for me. Like many universities, the University of Michigan was going to provide a home, or "official residence," for the Chancellor of its new campus. Therefore, Lois and I had no need to buy a house when we made the move. Having sold our home in Illinois, we had about $25,000 in cash from the sale and faced the question of what to do with the money. I was managing our portfolio, but I thought it might be good to have a professional manager handle this money. I saw an ad in the *Wall Street Journal* that would accept that small an amount of money for management, so I turned the money over to them. That was 1972 and you can imagine what happened to the money as we moved through the market collapse of 1973-74. I watched our balance in the account decline month after month and finally retrieved the money when the balance was about $14,000. In fact, I realized later that I was unfair in being so critical of the money management firm. The results were simply the product of what was happening in the financial markets in general. This was one of those lessons I have learned over sixty years. Do not expect money managers, mutual fund managers or other financial professionals to significantly outperform the market, especially over extended periods of time. They are subject to the same economic environment and market conditions as the rest of us.

The Michigan Years

Our years at Michigan were an amazing experience. The University of Michigan is a fine university, and the chance to help them develop a new campus was more than I could ever have contemplated. The land for the campus was a gift from the Ford Motor Company, whose world headquarters building was just across the road from the campus. The campus included Fair Lane, the home and estate of Henry Ford I. My responsibilities often brought me into contact with Ford executives, including several meetings with Henry Ford II when he was CEO. My father passed away just before we moved to Michigan, and given his work as a Ford mechanic and admirer of Henry I, I always regretted he did not live long enough to be aware of my close association with the company years later.

Robben Fleming was President of the University, and *Newsweek* had called him "the best university president in America." My years reporting to and working with him were learning years for me. He was an outstanding administrator, and his style affected all those who worked for and around him. Each Tuesday morning I would drive from Dearborn to Ann Arbor to attend cabinet meetings. His cabinet consisted of the university vice-presidents and two chancellors (Dearborn and Flint), and watching that group grapple with the problems of a large, complex university was for me like a graduate management course in a college of business.

The University of Michigan-Dearborn recruited an outstanding faculty and attracted many highly talented students, mostly from southeastern Michigan. The campus offered those who could not afford to move to Ann Arbor a chance to receive a University of Michigan quality education. The engineering program at UM-D was one of its most highly regarded academic offerings, primarily because of the co-op program which enabled students to get practical experience as part of their university education. In the years since I have left, the campus and grown and expanded its enrollment and program offerings while maintaining the high quality it has had from the beginning. The chancellors who followed me have provided strong leadership, and I am very pleased with the development of UM-D in recent years.

I had been there eight years when President Fleming left to become President of the Corporation for Public Broadcasting. I decided that was a good time for me to begin to look around at other positions. I interviewed for four different positions and was offered two. One of the positions was the presidency of the University of Nevada, Las Vegas. After thinking a lot about the two positions, Lois and I remembered our love of the Southwest and decided to take that offer. We were impressed with the energy and growth of Las Vegas and UNLV in particular.

Back to the Desert

Our family moved to Las Vegas in 1979, and we have lived here ever since. When we moved our oldest daughter, Karla, remained in Michigan to attend the University of Michigan, from which she graduated four years later. Karen and Greg moved with us to Las Vegas where both later graduated from high school.

UNLV was an exciting place to work. It was the largest university in the state, and the other university, the University of Nevada, Reno, was more than 400 miles away. Several academic programs already had a national reputation when I arrived. The College of Hotel Administration, taking advantage of its location in a world tourist center, was a superior program. It competed with its counterpart at Cornell as to which was the best hotel college in the nation. The fine arts and entertainment programs—theatre, dance, music, etc.—also had fine reputations. The programs all took advantage of their proximity to the Las Vegas Strip to raise private contributions, recruit part-time faculty from the "real world" of entertainment and to place their students in good jobs upon graduation. Our son, Greg, graduated from the College of Hotel Administration and immediately went to work for the Mirage Hotel.

UNLV was a young university, having been established in 1952, and it had few wealthy alumni. Therefore, it had to depend on local business and community leaders for private support. Fortunately there were a number who stepped up to the plate and made a big difference. Steve and Elaine Wynn were generous supporters, and Elaine devoted much time to campus fund raising matters when she was chair of the UNLV Foundation. The buildings on campus have names that identify some of those who shared generously with the campus—Ham, Beam, Thomas, Mack, Greenspun, Barrick, Lied.

Liberace not only had a home near the campus, he was an enthusiastic supporter of the campus music programs. Once when I was visiting the Liberace Museum I was surprised to find among the exhibits a framed letter that I had written thanking him for his continuing support of the campus.

I became president of UNLV in March, 1979. I was also appointed to a faculty position, professor of public administration, and I left the presidency to join the faculty full time in February, 1985. Two of the major projects that were completed while I was president were the establishment of the UNLV Foundation, the university's primary fund-raising arm, and the building of the Thomas and Mack Center, an 18,500 seat capacity events center, that became the home of our well known basketball team, the UNLV Runnin' Rebels. I considered these as somewhat parallel projects in that one strengthened the financial condition of the academic side of the campus and the other strengthened the financial condition of the athletic side of the campus.

One of the most popular programs initiated during my presidency was the Barrick Lecture Series. Marjorie Barrick, a prominent Las Vegas resident and philanthropist, funded the program with the stipulation that the lectures would always be free to the public. The series brought former U.S. presidents Jimmy Carter and Gerald Ford, prominent foreign speakers such as Mrs. Anwar Sadat and Mikhail Gorbachev, journalists such as Walter Cronkite, and scholars such as William Buckley and John Kenneth Galbraith to the campus. In other lecture series around the country, people often pay $15 to $75 a ticket to hear these speakers, but thanks to Mrs. Barrick's generosity, there is no cost for those who hear them at UNLV. It was very satisfying to serve as president of a university that was rapidly growing in both size and quality such as UNLV. After leaving office, I continued my career as a full time faculty member until I retired in 2000.

The university asked me to work on a number of projects after I joined the faculty. One that brought me great satisfaction was when President Carol Harter asked me to chair the committee to find the first dean of the university's new law school. I had a great committee representing the university and local legal community to work with, and we eventually identified four candidates for the job. From that list the president appointed Dick Morgan, then dean at Arizona State University, to be the founding dean. Dick did an outstanding job and moved the school to a position where it had a national reputation in a very short period of time.

I also served on the statewide committee that supervised the higher education retirement system. This involved regular meetings with the mutual fund and retirement companies that offered retirement options to faculty and staff. This was an opportunity for me to be involved in investing once again. I served several years as UNLV's representative on the committee, and then when I retired, I was appointed to be a retiree committee member. I enjoyed my time on the committee and hope my knowledge made a reasonable contribution to the committee's work.

Rediscovering the Worlds of Teaching and Investing

Many university governing boards, including the Nevada Board of Regents, have a policy of granting administrators who are leaving their positions a period of time to prepare to become full time faculty again. When I left the presidency the board granted me six months of leave time before I returned to the classroom. This gave me time for reading, choosing textbooks, gathering research materials and related activities. Two of the activities I undertook were taking a non-credit course and beginning a two-year program of studying for my Certified Financial Planner (CFP) designation.

I took a non-credit course offered by the university, Using the Computer for Stock Analysis, taught by Professor William Corney of the management department. I did not know Bill well at all, but we became close friends, and that friendship changed how I spent much of my time then, and how I spend it now. We met often over coffee to discuss stocks and financial matters, and about a year later, he suggested that we start a financial newsletter. That was the beginning of *No-Load Portfolios* (NLP) in 1986, a monthly newsletter that we have now published for over a quarter of a century. It began as a four-page publication and later expanded to eight. We publish the first Monday of each month with a focus on financial markets and the general economy, particularly on no-load mutual funds and exchange traded funds. Although both Professor Corney and I were full-time faculty when we started the newsletter, we usually used the last two weekends of the month to prepare for publication on the first Monday. We are retired now and able to spend more time with our newsletter. Hopefully it shows in the quality of the product.

A great advantage of *No-Load Portfolios* was that it forced us to do our homework. I read a lot of financial publications, which not only helped with the newsletter but also made me a better manager of my own portfolio. I also began attending financial seminars and conferences. Howard Ruff was one of the best known sponsors of financial conferences, and Lois and I attended several of his events, mainly in San Diego but sometimes in Phoenix or other southwestern cities. Other sponsors, such as Bob White and Investment Seminars International, presented their programs in Las Vegas, which made it easy for me to attend.

After going to these conferences over several years, I began to think that I could make as good a presentation as some of those I had been hearing. After approaching some of the seminar sponsors and asking if they would have room for me on their programs, several took a chance and invited me to speak at their Las Vegas conferences. Later those sponsors put me on their programs in Los Angeles, San Diego and Phoenix, the main locations for such conferences in this area. Eventually I was speaking at meetings throughout the U.S. and even a few overseas. I have spoken at most Las Vegas Money Shows for years and several of the Money Shows elsewhere that were sponsored by Intershow.

While speaking at a conference in Marbella, Spain in 1989, I met Dale Ennis, editor and publisher of *Canadian MoneySaver*, a first class, consumer oriented monthly read mainly by Canadians. Dale and I became good friends, and he asked me to write an occasional article for his magazine, which I did for over the next twenty-five years. He also invited me to speak at some of the conferences he sponsored. Most were in Canada, but I also had the opportunity to speak at Dale's conferences in the U.S., Costa Rica, Ireland and aboard cruise ships. Because of my association with Dale, we have a number of Canadian subscribers to *No-Load Portfolios*.

I also became active in the American Association of Individual Investors and purchased a life membership in 1983. I cannot say enough good about AAII. It is a great organization for individual investors, and its journal, newsletters, website and chapter meetings all provide quality objective information that is invaluable for the small (and not so small) investor. I am sure I paid less than $100 for my life membership. I have spoken to many AAII chapter meetings and their national convention through the years, and I often tell their members that the best investment I ever made was my AAII life membership.

Speaking at financial conferences, AAII and other investment club meetings gave me a chance to talk about *NLP* and distribute sample copies, and this helped increase our list of subscribers. The newsletter also benefitted from favorable commentary and high rankings by the financial press, especially *Hulbert's Financial Digest* and *Timer Digest.* Any favorable comments in the press, especially in *Hulbert's,* bring an immediate flurry of requests for sample copies and new subscriptions. The following are examples of the rankings.

Hulbert's Financial Digest

As of September 2010, among 28 monitored financial newsletters, *NLP* ranked third for portfolio performance on a risk- adjusted basis over a 15-year timespan.

As of January 2009, among 13 newsletters monitored over 5 years for gold timing, NLP ranked first on both an absolute return and a risk-adjusted return basis.

As of August 2008, among 41 monitored mutual fund newsletters published for more than 5 years, *NLP* ranked first on a risk-adjusted basis over 5 years.

Timer Digest

As of February 2009 *NLP* ranked third among stock timers over one year, second over six months and first over three months.

Runner Up for 2008 Timer of the Year award.

*NLP r*anked third among stock timers for 12 months through Dec 2007.

*NLP r*anked first among stock times for 12 months through Oct 2006.

Bill Corney deserves most of the credit for the high rankings. He has always taken the lead in deciding what buy/sell recommendations to make in the newsletter. We have benefited from the fact that our rankings have remained consistent through the years. Many newsletters make a high ranking once or twice and are not heard from again. As I write this early in 2012, *Hulbert's* has us ranked as follows:

Among the 37 mutual fund newsletters monitored for more than 5 years, *NLP* ranked seventh on a risk-adjusted basis.

Among the 34 mutual funds newsletters monitored for more than 10 years, *NLP* ranked fifth on a risk-adjusted basis.

Among the 30 mutual funds newsletters monitored for more than 15 years, *NLP* ranked third on a risk-adjusted basis.

Among the 50 financial newsletters of all types monitored for more than 20 years, *NLP* ranked fifth on a risk-adjusted basis.

In addition to the newsletter, Bill and I co-authored two books, *Worldwide Investing* and and *Managing Your TIAA-CREF Retirement Accounts.* The latter was mainly for college faculty and others whose retirement funds are invested with TIAA-CREF. Both books are now out of print.

Moving Into Retirement

After enjoying a thirty-eight year career in higher education, twenty-one of those years at UNLV, I retired from UNLV in 2000, although the adjustment was not a hard one to make. We continued to live in Las Vegas. In retirement I taught one course a year, a graduate seminar each fall semester on the subject, The Role of Government in Society. I also worked with the university in a number of other ways, including serving on master's and doctoral examining committees, assisting the UNLV Foundation with a number of fund-raising programs and helping out wherever I could. The university graciously provides me with an office even in my retirement years. Staying out of the way of the university's current president is something I have regarded as one of my major duties. The last thing a university president needs is to have former presidents criticizing and second-guessing what they are doing. I felt especially honored in 2006 when the Nevada Board of Regents presented me the Distinguished Nevadan Award, the highest honor they can give.

I continued my newsletter, along with writing and lecturing activities in retirement, and I had more time to devote to each. I also expanded my small financial planning practice. Although I had completed my Certified Financial Planner certification in 1988, I had only a small practice with few clients. Most of those I worked with were faculty who wanted advice on their retirement plan. Since I was in the same plan, I was able to help them without a lot of homework on my part. Retirement enabled me to expand my practice somewhat, including a number of non-university clients.

Retirement also gave Lois and me the opportunity to do more things we enjoyed. We made more trips to visit children, grandchildren and other family members, mainly in Arizona, Iowa and Missouri. We both enjoy cruising, and we have taken cruises in many parts of the world. We continued our work with First Presbyterian Church, and we each had our own community groups with which we worked. I was in the Rotary Club, and she was active in PEO and the Assistance League of Las Vegas.

I have been luckier in life than I could possibly deserve. Loving parents, a beautiful and wonderful wife, very able children and absolutely perfect (of course!) grandchildren have brought a lot of joy to my life. Being as educator as my primary profession, I have considered myself to be fortunate to always have positions where I enjoyed the work I was doing. I also enjoyed my investing and money management activities, but they were never my full-time work. That is what makes this book different. Many financial professionals have written books about their experiences, but they were usually people who had devoted their careers to the world of finance. I write as an individual investor who always had other responsibilities and duties. I hope many of my readers will be in the same situation, average people with professional, family and other responsibilities who can only devote a portion of their time to their investing interests.

Chapter 3
Asset Allocation:
The Single Most Important Investment Strategy

If you have read investment books, talked to financial planners or brokers, or attended financial seminars, you have heard it said time and again that asset allocation is the single most important investment strategy. The reason it is repeated so often is because it is true. Nothing will influence your success as an investor more than how you have your investments distributed among the various asset categories. Some have referred to it as applying the old proverb, "Don't put all your eggs in one basket," to the world of investing. Ray Lucia, the highly respected investment talk show host, talks about placing your money in different buckets, each with a different investment purpose. William Bernstein, one of the most authoritative and prolific writers on the subject, defines asset allocation as the process of dividing up one's securities among broad asset classes, i.e., foreign and domestic stocks and foreign and domestic bonds (*The Intelligent Asset Allocator*, 2001). Figure 3.1 on the next page provides examples of typical asset categories.

Many people consider there to be only three basic categories: stocks, fixed income and cash. It is common to read in the financial pages that some large investment firms, perhaps J.P. Morgan or First Boston, are now recommending an asset allocation of 65% stocks, 25% fixed income and 10% cash. They often do not mention real estate, precious metals, commodities or any other categories, just the three.

Figure 3.1
Typical Asset Allocation Categories

Stocks	*Real Estate*
Large-Cap	Residential
Mid-Cap	Single
Small-Cap	Multi-family
Sector	Commercial
Financials, Tech.	Industrial
Consumers, etc.	International
International	REITs
Regional (Europe, Asia,	
Latin America, etc.)	
Emerging market	
Single country	

Bonds and Fixed Income	*Commodities*
U.S. Treasuries	Comprehensive Funds
2-yr, 5-yr, 10-yr, 20-yr, etc.	Energy
Inflation Protected	Oil, coal, Natural
Municipal Bonds	Gas, etc
State, County,Schools, etc.	Agriculture
Corporate Bonds	Cattle, Wheat, Soy
Short, Iintermediate &	Beans, Orange
Long-Term Bonds	Juice, etc.
Investment Grade	Natural Resources
High Yield	Water, Timber, etc.
Bonds of Foreign Countries	

Cash and Cash Equivalents	*Precious Metals*
Checking Accounts	Bullion
Savings Accounts	Gold, Silver
Certificates of Deposit	Coins
Money Market Funds	Certificates

I am not sure when I first discovered the concept of asset allocation. I expect it was sometime in the 1970s when I was first becoming familiar with the writings of Burt Malkiel. I certainly remember when the stock market lost about half its value during the downturn of 1973-74. I quickly learned one of the basic principles of asset allocation, the money I did *not* have invested in the stock market was not subject to the wide fluctuations of the market. For example, the prices of bonds, real estate and cash equivalents all had price fluctuations that were not correlated with the stock market.

The idea of asset allocation was first discussed among a group of scholars at the University of Chicago in the 1950s. Their work evolved into what became known as Modern Portfolio Theory (MPT). One of the group was Harry Markowitz, a graduate student, whose research was some of the earliest on this subject. He was especially interested in the fact that there were varying correlations among the price movements of different types of investments. They did not all move up or down in price at the same time. He noted that risk is not reduced by the individual holdings in a portfolio but by how the varying categories of investments were correlated with one another. In 1990 Markowitz was one of three who received the Nobel Prize for Economics for their work on asset allocation.

One of my more embarrassing moments came because of that Nobel Prize. A few years ago, I was invited to speak to the Portland, Oregon chapter of the American Association of Individual Investors. Prior to my coming, they asked me to give them a short description of my presentation that could be used for publicity purposes. In the statement I sent them, I wrote that one of the topics I would be discussing was asset allocation. I added that this topic is so important that research on the subject had won the Nobel Economics Award in 1990. About two weeks before the presentation, I received a phone call from the chapter president, who was very apologetic. He said that their publicity chairman had misread my statement and had issued a news release saying that I had done the research that won the Nobel Prize in 1990. I am not usually nervous before speaking, but I was very uneasy as I went to that meeting. I thought about all those people believing they were going to hear a Nobel winner speak to them, and they were going to end up with me. However, everything went very well. The president did a very good job of explaining the mistake to the group, and they could not have been more gracious in welcoming me and listening to my presentation. I jokingly told them that I wanted extra copies of the news story to take home and to show my grandchildren because it was the closest I would ever come to winning a Nobel!

How Important Is It?

Just how important is asset allocation? Is it really the most important investment strategy? To answer that question, it is important to remember that we use asset allocation for just one reason—because we cannot predict the future. If we could predict the future, nothing would make less sense than diversifying our investments. If we could predict with certainty that stocks will return 12% over the next year, bonds 9%, real estate 8%, and precious metals 5%, we would want to put all of our money in the 12% category. We would want nothing to do with the investments paying 9%, 8%, or 5%. It is precisely because neither we nor anyone else, including your favorite guru, can predict the future that we use asset allocation.

There are three factors that determine our investment returns (positive or negative). The first is security selection. We make a decision to buy Pepsi instead of Coke, Ford instead of General Motors, Hilton rather than Marriott, etc. Obviously our decision of what to buy and sell affects our investment returns. Second, returns are impacted by timing. We decide when to buy and sell. Our decision may be based on a company's earnings, a computer program, a charting program, the recommendation of a newsletter writer or even a popular rule of thumb, such as "sell in May and go away." Third, asset allocation affects our investment return. Our investment success is clearly influenced by how we distribute our money among the various asset categories.

Among the three (stock selection, timing, and asset allocation), which is most important in determining our investment return? David Swenson, well known for his work as manager of the Yale University endowment funds and author of the best seller, *Unconventional Success* (2005), makes an interesting argument on the importance of asset allocation. He contends that asset allocation accounts for *more than 100%* of an investor's positive return. How can that be? He points to studies which show that individual investors usually have a net loss from their stock selection and timing decisions. Attempts to time the market are almost always losers, and individuals are up against big odds on stock selection as they compete with the information and research power of mutual funds, hedge funds, and other institutional investors. Therefore, if an individual has a positive return, it is because his or her asset allocation has more than made up for the net losses in timing and security selection. Whether or not you agree with Swensen's rather unique reasoning, there is a broad consensus that asset allocation is by far the most important of the three. I have seen studies that suggest that asset allocation accounts for 75% to 80% of portfolio return. Other studies say the number is above 90%. Whatever the number, it is clear that no investment decision deserves more of your serious attention than asset allocation.

Developing Your Plan

All of us have an allocation plan, either one we develop deliberately or one developed by accident. If every dollar you have to your name is in a checking account, then your asset allocation is 100% in cash. If you then open a savings account, your allocation is still 100% cash. If your brother-in-law gives you a hot tip on a stock and you buy it, your allocation is now split between stocks and cash. This is exactly the wrong way to develop an asset allocation plan. The right way should include the following steps.

Developing a plan calls for deciding ahead of time how you want to distribute your financial assets among the categories available to you. Your task is to decide what strategy best meets your needs. There is no cookie cutter one-size-fits-all approach. Keep in mind that the purpose of asset allocation is not so much to increase return as it is to reduce risk. You do that by allocating your assets among categories that have little price movement correlation, i.e., they do not go up and down at the same time.

Generally, the higher your risk tolerance, the higher the portion of your financial assets you want to have in stocks. Also, the longer the time you have to invest, the more you will want to invest in the stock category. For example, in your retirement accounts you may want 85% or more of your funds in stocks when you are in your 20s or 30s, but only 25% or 30% as you approach retirement age. The same is true if you are investing to send a child to college. When the child is three years old you want the investments to be primarily in stocks, but a much lower amount should be in stocks when he or she is just two or three years away from college. You don't want a market downturn just as the child is graduating from high school and with no time for a market recovery before they enter college.

There is an old rule of thumb that says subtract your age from 100 and you will have the percentage of your portfolio that should be in stock. Using this rule, a 34 year old would allocate 66% of her invest-ment funds to stocks. At age 55, the number comes down to 45%. Of course, this is just what it says it is, a rule of thumb. It makes no allow-ance for your risk tolerance, your employment situation, your financial obligations, and other characteristics; however, it is a place to start.

Once when I was speaking to an investment seminar, one of the attendees challenged me forcefully on this point. He said, "I am 70 years old. I have a secure retirement income. My mortgage is paid off and the college educations of all my children are paid for. Now is the time I want to take some real risks with my investing." I pointed out to him that the main reason we tend to want less risk in our portfolios as we get older is because, in case of a stock market disaster, we have less time to recover than a 40 or 50 year old would. Many investors remember sharp stock losses during the energy crisis of 1973-74, the bursting of the technology stock bubble of 2000-02, and the real estate bubble of 2007-09. It takes time to recover from that kind of loss. Nevertheless, the gentleman's comment makes the point that there is no single plan for everyone.

In working with young faculty on their financial planning needs, I have discovered that many of them are far too conservative in funding their retirement accounts. Even though they are in the 20s or 30s, they often have 50% or more of their retirement funds in a money market account. When asked why, they refer to the tech bubble or the real estate bubble. I point out to them that they are investing for 30 or 40 years and should not be overly influenced by what happened recently. It is often said there has never been a fifteen year period when stocks have not gone up. That is not precisely true, as discussed in the next chapter, but the point to be made is that young investors should not have most of their money in a money market fund.

I suggest you use at least the three basic asset categories when deciding on an asset allocation: stocks, bonds and cash. The simplest of portfolios might look like this:

Stocks	60%
Bonds	35%
Cash	5%

Burt Malkiel, in the 2011 edition of his classic, *Random Walk Down Wall Street*, says that if you owned a portfolio of 60% in an all stock index fund and 40% in an all bond index fund beginning in 1995, and you had rebalanced annually through 2009, you would have achieved a 10% compound return during that period. This is in spite of the fact that those years included both of the bear markets beginning in 2000 and 2007. This is an example of what I mean when I say the most effective investment strategies are also often the easiest to understand and implement.

Malkiel's example includes two categories, stocks and bonds. My example above includes a third category, a small allocation to cash. I think it is good to have such a category, mainly to serve as a parking place for cash and to provide some flexibility when it comes time to rebalance. It is not a big issue, and you can decide whether you want to include a cash category in your portfolio. As your portfolio grows larger and more complex, including more of the sub-categories shown in Figure 3.1, it is more likely you will want to include a cash category. Also, when interest rates are high, there will be times when you will want to own savings accounts or money market funds because they provide some income at very little risk.

As your portfolio grows, you may well want to include more categories, such as precious metals, commodities, or currencies in your holdings. Not many years ago it was almost impossible for the small individual investor to invest in these areas, but the coming of exchange-traded funds has changed all that. Today if you want your portfolio to include coal, oil, natural gas, agricultural commodities, gold, silver or even a particular foreign currency, there are ETFs that will enable you to do so. Figure 3.2 provides examples. Here is where you can use your own knowledge and experience to strengthen your holdings. If you work in the agribusiness field, such as farming, farm products processing or farm equipment manufacturing, you have an advantage in choosing agriculture related ETFs for your investments. If you travel overseas frequently in your work and have a good feel for the value of the dollar against foreign currencies, you might choose a foreign currency ETF, perhaps the Euro or Swiss franc. If you are like me, not an expert in a given field, but you want to include commodities in your asset allocation, you can choose among several ETFs that hold a wide variety of different kinds of commodities.

If you would like some help in developing an asset allocation plan, there is plenty available. There are good books like Bernstein's *The Intelligent Asset Allocator* (2001) and Daniel R. Solin's, *The Smartest Investment Book You'll Ever Read* (2006). Solon's book includes an Asset Allocation Questionnaire (Appendix A) that provides a set of questions you can answer that will give you an idea of what an appropriate allocation plan for you might look like. Virtually every mutual fund website includes a section on asset allocation with tools to help you make decisions. Among my favorite websites with sections on this topic are morningstar.com, yahoo.com, and cnnmoney.com.

Example Portfolios

While someone else's allocation is unlikely to be exactly right for you, you can get helpful ideas by seeing how others have built their portfolios. Several portfolios are presented below, not to be recommendations, but to provide alternatives for you to consider. The first is a portfolio of my own. This is a five fund portfolio that constitutes a part of my retirement accounts. It looks like this:

S&P500 Index Fund	20%
Russell 2000 Index Fund	20%
International Index Fund	20%

REIT Index fund	20%
Intermediate Bond Index Fund	20%

One advantage of this portfolio is its simplicity. Each fund has the same allocation, 20%. I rebalance annually, a process that is very simple with this portfolio. I am thinking about adding a commodities fund to the portfolio.

Figure 3.2
Investment Products to Add
Diversification to Your Portfolio

Inflation Protected Securities
iShares Barkley's TIPs (TIP)
Vanguard Infl. Protected (VIPSX)
Fidelity Infl. Protected (FIPSX)
www.treasurydirect.gov

Foreign Currency ETFs
Euro(FXE), Australian $ (FXA)
Pound (FXB), Canadian $ (FXC)
Yen (FXY), Mexican Peso (FXM)
Swedish Kroner (FXS),
Swiss Franc (FXF)

Commodities
iPath DJ AIG Comm. (DJP)
Powershares DB Comm. (DBC)
TRowePrice New Era (PRNEX)
Pimco Real Return (PRNEX)
Oppenheimer Real Asset (DRAAX)
First Trust Water (FIW)
US Natural Gas (UNG)
US Oil (USO)
Mkt. Vectors Agribusiness (MOO)
Mkt. Vectors Coal (KOL)
Claymore Timber (CUT)

Real Estate
Am. Cent. RE (REACX)
Fidelity RE (FRESX)
iShares DJ Real Estate (IYR)
iShares Cohen &Steers (ICF)
Vanguard REIT (VNQ)

Bonds
iSh. Barkley's 1-3 yr (SHY)
iSh. Barkley's 7-10 yr (IEF)
iSh Barkley's 20+ yr (TLT)
iSh. Barkley's Aggregate (AGG)

Precious Metals
DJ Gold Shares (GLD)
Comex Gold Trust (IAU)
Am. Cent. Global Gold (AVGGX)

Inverse Movement Funds
ProShares Short Dow (DOG)
Proshares Short SP500 (SH)
Proshares Short QQQ (PSQ)
Ryder Inverse 2X SP500 (RSW)

The following allocation examples come from the morning-star.com website, mentioned above as one of my favorites:

Stocks	Conservative Portfolio	Balanced Portfolio	Aggressive Portfolio
Large Value		10%	5%
Large Blend	15%	10%	5%
Large Growth		10%	15%
Mid/Small-Cap	8%	10%	25%
International	5%	5%	15%
Real Estate	5%	5%	10%
Bonds			
Short/Intermediate	30%	20%	5%
Inflation-Protected	20%	15%	5%
High Yield		5%	5%
Foreign	5%	5%	5%
Cash	12%	5%	5%

One thing I have learned by watching others as well as myself is that the more categories you have in a portfolio, the less likely you are to rebalance on a regular basis. It's just easier to do with a few portfolio holdings than with many. Since rebalancing is at the heart of asset allocation, keep the total number of securities in your portfolio to a level where you will have the discipline to rebalance regularly. For some that number may be only five. For others, it may be ten, twelve, twenty or more. On this point, know thyself!

Daniel Solin, in his book listed above, suggests a very simple three fund portfolio using Vanguard funds. He lets you choose among four different levels of risk.

Vanguard	Low Risk	Medium/Low Risk	Medium/High Risk	High Risk
Total Stock	14%	28%	42%	56%
Total International	6%	12%	18%	24%
Total Bond	80%	60%	40%	20%

Solin notes that you could build this same portfolio using Fidelity index funds. With just three funds rebalancing becomes simple and straightforward. Solin makes a strong case for index funds, a point with which I agree and discuss in more detail in Chapter 6.

William Bernstein, mentioned above, recommends an aggressive portfolio that looks like this:

10% S&P500   10% International small cap
10% US small cap   10% Emerging markets
10% REITS   10% Precious metals
10% International large cap   30% Short term bonds

Bernstein says the portfolio is only for the "hardiest of souls and the most independent of thinkers."

Finally, I will describe a portfolio that I created but do not recommend for most people. I strongly believe that to achieve long-term growth, a portfolio should include a reasonable allocation to stocks. However, I had a financial planning client come to me not long ago who wanted absolutely nothing to do with the stock market. I built an all bond portfolio for him and later discussed it in two articles in the July and September, 2010 issues of NLP. Here is the portfolio:

Intermediate Term Bond Fund	40%
GNMA Fund	15%
Intermed. Term Investment Grade	15%
Corporate High Yield Fund	10%
Inflation Protected Bond Fund	10%
Money Market Fund	10%

I pointed out to the client that he could add other non-stock holdings to his portfolio, including precious metals, currencies, commodities and real estate investment trusts if he wants to do so. If his aversion to the stock market, however, is because of a general aversion to risk, then he should probably stick just to bond holdings instead of adding these other high risk categories to his investments. I included this portfolio to show the wide range of asset allocations. I still recommend that most investors should own some stocks most of the time. Having reviewed all the ideas above, your task is to create an asset allocation strategy that best meets your individual investment needs.

Fifty-fifty and Forget It

Having spent most of my professional life in a university setting, most of my retirement funds are with the Teachers Insurance and Annuity/College Retirement Equities Fund (TIAA/CREF). TIAA was created in 1918 by the Carnegie Foundation and the Carnegie Corporation to provide a retirement fund mainly for the nation's college and university faculty and staff. A major goal of this new firm was to provide portability as faculty moved from university to university. Up to that time many faculty who had retirement plans at all were in state plans that they could not take with them as they made career moves. TIAA provided a fixed income option that gave participants a stable income during their retirement years. CREF, established in 1952, offered a market based option that provided a variable income during retirement, fluctuating annually depending on the movement of the stock market. Today TIAA/CREF offers a wide choice of stock and bond funds, but for many years each offered only the one fund.

Many faculty members in those earlier days had little knowledge of or interest in the world of investing, and they would just split their contributions equally between the two funds, making no other changes through the years. It was common on college campuses for this to be known as the "fifty-fifty and forget it" strategy. Faculty would contribute 50% to each and forget about it until they neared retirement. Interestingly, many retired faculty will tell you today that this strategy served them very well. They have enjoyed a secure retirement with part of their income being stable and guaranteed and the remainder growing through the years as the stock market has experienced long term gains. I think the lesson to be learned here is that even the simplest of allocation plans is better than no plan at all.

Rebalancing

The lynchpin of successful asset allocation is a program of regular rebalancing. This is the process of bringing your portfolio back into line with your asset allocation plan. If you have a plan to have 60% in stocks, and the stock market has had a good year, you may find your portfolio has grown to 68% in stocks by year end. You will need to sell sufficient stocks to bring the portfolio back in line with the plan, and use the money raised from the sale to add to the categories that are now below your goals. If the balances are only 2% or 3% off, I would not bother with rebalancing, but if they are 5% or more away from their goals, rebalancing usually makes sense. Rebalancing is counter-intuitive and our emotions often urge us not to do it. We are selling winners and buying losers, and it is no fun to talk about that at a cocktail party. Nevertheless, rebalancing strengthens our investment holdings. Remember that it does not require selling all or even most of your winners. You keep most of your winners and only sell enough to bring your plan back into balance.

How often should you rebalance? Most market analysts seem to think once a year is enough, and I am in agreement with that. Some investors want to rebalance semi-annually or quarterly, but I am aware of no research that suggests there is much to be gained from that. Bernstein recommends rebalancing "no more than once a year," suggesting it may be appropriate to wait 18 months or two years on occasion. Richard Jenkins, editor of msnmoney.com, says rebalancing should be done "at least once a year." Alexander Green, author of *The Gone Fishin' Portfolio* (2005), says disciplining yourself to rebalance on a regular basis is more important than exactly when you do it. My recommendation is that you rebalance annually, but there is nothing magic about that.

If you are investing taxable dollars, when you rebalance can make a difference. I suggest rebalancing around year end. If you need to sell securities to rebalance, and those sales will generate capital gains, you should wait until January to make the sales. That way you will not have capital gains tax to pay for 15 months, April 15 of the following year. On the other hand, if your sales involve capital losses, you can sell in December and take the losses on your current year tax bill. If you are rebalancing inside a retirement or other tax protected account, it doesn't matter when you sell. Your gains or losses are not subject to taxation.

A Big Mistake—Saved by Asset Allocation

A few years ago an event occurred where asset allocation provided important protection for my portfolio. In the early 1990s, as mentioned earlier, I joined with Dr. Bill Stephan and several other Las Vegas residents to form a new bank, Commercial Bank of Nevada. I served as vice-chairman of the board of the bank. The bank did well, and about a decade later we sold the bank to Colonial Bank, a southeastern regional bank with headquarters in Montgomery, Alabama. When we sold the bank, we were paid not in cash but in shares of Colonial Bank. In the boom years of the early 2000s, the bank did well, the stock moved up nicely, and my portfolio benefitted accordingly. Then when the real estate collapse occurred, Colonial was heavily invested in Florida real estate loans. The bank was hit hard and its stocks fell sharply. It continued to struggle, and in 2009 the FDIC stepped in and took over the bank. Like other shareholders, I was caught by surprise. I knew the bank was having difficulties, but I did not expect an FDIC takeover, meaning the price of the shares went to $0. Perhaps if I had done my homework more thoroughly I might have seen the action coming, but I did not.

My portfolio felt the harsh impact of the governmental takeover, but there was one intervening factor—asset allocation—that greatly softened the impact of the blow. I have never wanted any one stock to constitute more than 10% of my total portfolio, preferably much less. Each year when I rebalance, in addition to adjusting my asset categories, I make the adjustments necessary to reduce holdings in any stock approaching or surpassing the 10% figure. Therefore, in the early 2000s, when Colonial stock was enjoying major gains, I was selling some stock regularly to keep my portfolio within the 10% limit. The stock sales in the good years significantly reduced the effect of the losses when the stock value became worthless. I credit my asset allocation policy with forcing me into the discipline that involved major selling in the good years. Without that discipline, I would have suffered considerably greater losses.

Letting Others Do It for You

One approach to asset allocation is to own funds that will do the rebalancing for you. There are a number of companies that now offer "target date" funds. The funds are designed primarily for retirement accounts, and they offer different funds for different target years—2020, 2030, 2035, etc. The idea is that the investor chooses the fund that most closely corresponds to the year when they plan to retire. The fund strategy is to invest more aggressively in the early years and then to get increasingly more conservative as the retirement target year approaches. For example, a 2035 fund might have 80% to 90% of its portfolio in stocks in 2015, and it would gradually reduce its allocation to stocks over time.

Several firms offer such funds. Examples would be the T.Rowe Price Retirement Funds, the fidelity Freedom Funds and the Vanguard Target Retirement Funds. Each company will have its own idea about asset allocation. In 2011 in the portfolios for 2040, T. Rowe Price and Vanguard both have 90% allocated to the stocks while the allocation for Fidelity was 84%. For the 2025 funds, T. Rowe Price had an 80% allocation to stocks. The figure for Vanguard was 74% and for Fidelity it was 70%. There are other companies that offer good target date funds. This is an area where you have an opportunity for comparison shopping.

Target date funds are not for everyone, and my guess is they would not be a good choice for you. If you are reading this book, you probably have a genuine interest in investments, and most serious investors will want to make their own asset allocation decisions for their portfolios. All of us, however, know people—siblings, children, friends, coworkers, etc.—who would not read an investment book or attend a financial seminar if their lives depended on it. They just could not care less about money management or investing. Nevertheless, many of these people will have a 401k or similar plan where they work, and many of those plans offer target date funds as one of their options. If you could just get these individuals, who might be willing to listen to your advice, to make the one-time decision to choose a target date fund for their retirement accounts and to regularly invest in those accounts, you could make a great improvement in their future lives. A professional fund manager is making their asset allocation decisions for them, and their accounts will become increasingly conservative as they near retirement.

Another good use of these target date funds is for the individual who has several small accounts to manage, perhaps for loved ones. If you have several children, each of them has given you grandchildren and you are in the position to help each of them financially, you may be contributing to eight, ten or more individual accounts. It is likely you may not have the time to make decisions for each of the accounts. Target date funds might be a good solution to your problem. If you are saving to help with education expenses, pick a target date fund that coincides as closely as possible with the time the child or grandchild will be entering college, and invest in that fund for them. If you are a serious individual investor, you will want to make your own asset allocation decisions for your portfolio. If you are helping others who have little interest in finance, target date funds may be a good instrument for you to use.

Chapter 4
Making Time Your Friend

If someone told you they had an investment for you that has no risk and is guaranteed to double your money, you might ask, "What's the catch?" The catch in the statement is that it did not include the element of time. If you could buy U.S. government bonds paying 4% and hold them for eighteen years, you would double your money while incurring virtually no risk other than inflation risk. Most of us may not want to hold government bonds for eighteen years, but it points out the crucial role of time in investing.

The fundamental message for investors where time is concerned is that the longer your time horizon, the more successful your investing is likely to be. Warren Buffett likes to say that his time horizon is "forever." He does not plan to ever sell what he owns. His wealth is such that he can make such a statement. There is no point in the future where he will have to sell some of his assets in order to buy a house, pay tuition, create a retirement plan, etc. It could also be said that large foundations such as those serving universities or charitable organizations have a "forever" horizon. They do not ever plan to spend all their funds. They will likely spend their interest and dividend income, and they must comply with laws that regulate them by spending a certain part of their principal. Beyond that they plan to be a permanent financial resource for the institution they serve.

Some individuals are fortunate enough to have some "forever" money. Most of us try to have money set aside to meet certain goals and time horizons such as to buy a home or vacation condo, pay education costs, start a business, create an adequate retirement fund, etc. A few people are fortunate enough to have all their goals funded, including emergency funds, and still have money they believe will never needed in their lifetimes. They can treat this money as if it has no specific time horizon, i.e. "forever' money. It will eventually go to their heirs, their church or synagogue, their university or whatever cause they have a special interest in. In the meantime, they can invest it as if it has no specific time horizon.

There is a Wall Street proverb that says successful investing comes from *time in* the market, not *timing of* the market. The fact that we cannot time the market is a recurring theme of this book. It is one lesson I have learned well over sixty years. At this point, let's look at using your time in the market effectively. We will focus on four issues that relate to making time your friend in the market: (1) starting early; (2) investing regularly; (3) using dollar averaging; and (4) benefitting from compound interest.

Starting Early

Whatever your time horizon for a specific investment goal, the earlier you begin investing to meet it, the better. Consider the goal of retiring at age 65, and how two individuals, Mr. Earlystarter and Mr.Stickwithit, addressed that goal:

Mr. Earlystarter is enthusiastic and gets started early by investing $5000 annually in his individual retirement account beginning at age 21. He continues to invest $5000 every year for fifteen years. At age 35, however, he becomes distracted. Perhaps he is getting married, starting a business or buying a home, but for whatever reason he stops his annual contributions. He never makes another contribution to his IRA through all his working years.

Mr. Stickwithit is preoccupied through his twenties and early thirties. He is doing other things and has little time for investing. Finally, at age 35, he gets serious about planning for retirement and opens an IRA. He starts investing $5000 annually in his IRA and loyally sticks with it for thirty years until he retires at age 65.

Which of these individuals will have the most money in his retirement account at the age of 65, the early starter who invests for fifteen years or the consistent investor who invests for thirty years? Assuming a net annual return of 6%, at age 65, Mr. Earlystarter will have an IRA balance of $668,428, while Mr. Sticktoit's balance will be $395, 291. What happened? We see in this example the value of starting early. After fifteen years of investing, beginning at age 21 and continuing to age 35, Mr. Earlystarter had an IRA balance of $116,380. This is enough to produce an annual return on the investment of more than $5000, so the account itself creates annual payments of over $5000 even though the IRA owner is contributing nothing.

These figures raise the question of a third mythical investor, Mr. Doitall, who not onlystarts at age 21 but has the persistence to keep investing for 45 years. What would his account look like at age 65. If Mr. Doitall makes $5000 annual contributions from age 21 to age 65, he would have an account balance of $1,063,718 as he enters retirement. Not bad. These calculations do not reflect the real world, where most 21 year olds do not have $5000 to invest annually in an IRA, and the significant impact of inflation over a period of more than four decades is not taken into consideration. Also, the numbers do not reflect the fact that wise investors will increase their annual IRA contributions as they get older and their incomes increase. However, the numbers do show the importance of starting early, whatever one's investment goals may be.

Investing Regularly

The IRA example above illustrates the importance not only of starting early but also of investing regularly. Sometimes this happens automatically if you have a 401k, 403b or similar account. Each pay period both your contributions and your employer's will go directly to the account. You do not have to do anything to make it happen.

You can make this work in other accounts as well. Many brokers and mutual fund companies will provide a service whereby they automatically deduct an amount you specify from your bank account each month or quarter and invest it directly in the fund or funds you have chosen. You might, for example, choose one stock mutual fund and one bond mutual fund and have your investments split evenly between the two.

If you have the self-discipline to do this on your own, you do not need an automated system to do it for you. You can just make regular periodic investments monthly, quarterly or in whatever time frame you choose. If you do this you need to remove emotion from the process as much as possible and not second-guess yourself with each periodic investment. You do not want to say, "I'll skip investing this month because I think the market will be lower next month," or "I'm going to skip my stock fund for a while and put all my investment in my bond fund because I think interest rates will go down and push the price of my bond fund up." It is the regularity of your investing and not you trying to outguess the direction of the market that makes this a successful way to invest. The illustration below makes this point.

How the World's Dumbest Investor Got Rich

To illustrate the power of investing regularly, let's assume an investor invests $1000 annually for twenty years. He purchases an index fund that tracks the Dow Jones Industrial Average. His problem is that every year for twenty years he manages to make his investment on the worst day possible, the day on which the Dow hits its high for that year. I have called him the world's dumbest investor but perhaps he is just the world's unluckiest investor. He invests his first $1000 on April 27, 1981, the day the market hit its high for that year. He continues investing $1000 annually for the next nineteen years, making his twentieth investment on January 14, 2000. At this point he has invested a total of $20,000, but his portfolio balance is $125,065. This represents an annual return of 16.7%. During that twenty year period dividends averaged 3.3%. I have assumed that 1.3% would be needed for items such as transaction costs and annual fund expenses. Therefore, I assumed there was a net 2.0% annual dividend income to be reinvested each year.

A critic might question the choice of that particular twenty-year period, and that would be a fair criticism. After all, the period 1981-2000 was generally bullish for the market, and especially during the tech stock boom of the late 1990s, stocks moved up sharply. So let's assume our investor continued investing for another ten years, 2001-10. Remember that this was a period when the market went essentially nowhere for a decade.

It was a period that included both the tech stock and the real estate busts. It has been called a "lost decade" for the stock market, but our investor did not do too badly during this time. He continued to invest $1000 annually. Each year his investment was made on the worst day possible, the day the Dow hit its high for the year. At the end of the decade he had invested another $10,000 but his portfolio had grown from $125,065 to $161,944. His portfolio hit a high of almost $183,000 in 2007 before falling to $143,646 in 2009, and then bouncing back to close the decade at over $160,000. This represented an annual return of just 1.9% for that decade, but for the full thirty-year period, he had an average return of 9.2%, and this was a period of three decades that included every possible stock market action—bull markets, bear markets, flat markets, booms, busts, etc. By investing regularly, even though his timing was terrible, our investor did pretty well. Maybe he wasn't so dumb after all. Of course, if he had invested his $1,000 on the first business day of each year, instead of the day when the Dow hit its highest point, his return would have been even higher.

Dollar Averaging

One reason our investor did well was because his $1000 annual investment bought more shares in years when the Dow went down. This is the application of the basic principle of dollar averaging. If individuals invest the same amount on a regular basis, they will buy more shares when the price is low, as shown here:

Amount Invested	Price	Shares Bought	Shares Owned
$20	$5.00	4	4
$20	$4.00	5	9

$20	$8.00	2.5	11.5
$20	$10.00	2	13.5
$20	$8.00	2.5	16.00

Amount invested: $100
Value of investment: $128 ($8.00 x 16 shares)
Average price of share during this period: $7.00
Average price paid for a share: $6.25

In this case the investor invests $20 monthly for five months. When the share price was $10, the investor bought only two shares, but when the share price was $4, the $20 investment buys five shares. Although the average price for a share over the five-month period was $7.00, the dollar averaging investor actually paid only $6.25 per share because the lower the price, the more shares $20 would buy.

This is a good way for an investor to get started. Helping a son, daughter or friend begin a program of investing monthly in a good mutual fund can introduce them to the stock market and the idea of regular investing. There are a number of mutual fund companies that offer the opportunity to invest as little as $50 monthly. The list of funds changes constantly, but you can screen for funds with low minimum investments at any good financial website. As an alternative you can call your favorite mutual fund company and ask them what funds they offer with low periodic investment amounts. For several years in the 1970s and 1980s I invested in two mutual funds in this way, with one additional twist; Any month in which the price of the fund had fallen at least 10% from the prior month, I doubled my investment for that month only. This happened infrequently, but when it did it gave my share value a boost. Most of us dollar average with our retirement accounts whether we realize it or not. During my working years I directed each month's contributions (both mine and my employer's) to the same set of TIAA-CREF funds. When I would be frustrated watching the stock market and my stock funds decline, I would remind myself that my contributions were buying more shares during those times. In the long run, time was my friend, and the market always recouped its losses.

Compound Interest

The final component in making time the investor's friend is compound interest. This is simply the idea that leaving your interest payments in an account as they accrue means that future interest payments will be made on both the original principal and the accrued interest. It also applies to plans in which you leave your dividends to be reinvested to buy more shares of stock. Some people quote Albert Einstein as saying that compound interest is the "most powerful force in the universe." Others say that he called it "the eighth wonder of the world." I am not sure he said either of these things, but whether he did or not, they point to the power of compound interest as an ally of the investor. I prefer a statement attributed to Benjamin Franklin. I do not know if he ever used the term, compound interest, but he is credited with saying, "Money makes money and the money money makes, makes more money." That is about as good a definition of the term as I have seen.

Compound interest is often associated with the "rule of 72," which says that, if you divide your interest rate into 72, you will get the number of years it takes to double your money. For example, if you have an investment paying you 6%, it will take twelve years to double your investment. If the interest rate is 9%, it will take eight years to double. As time passes, if you have left your interest and dividends to be reinvested, it will greatly contribute to your investment success. That is what compound interest is all about.

Inflation: When Time Is Not Your Friend

The other side of the compound interest coin is that time can erode the value of your investments through the impact of inflation. Any time you make investment projections, especially for long periods of time such as retirement, it is essential that you consider the impact of inflation. The rule of 72 works in reverse here. If you have calculated that you will receive $60,000 annually when you retire in twenty-four years, assuming a 3% inflation rate, the rule of 72 tells you that your retirement income will be worth $30,000 in today's dollars.

There are a number of ways to calculate inflation. You can buy a financial calculator ($50-$75), and it is easy to learn how to build inflation assumptions into your investment planning. If you use a computer regularly, you can use a spreadsheet program such as Excel to help you. Probably the easiest way is to use the tools available on many financial websites. The major financial websites as well as those of the large mutual fund companies usually have special sections that will calculate the impact of inflation for you. All you have to do is enter your numbers into their program, and the computer will do the work for you.

Chapter 5
Mutual Funds and ETFs:
The Best Investments for Most of Us

As the chapter title indicates, I believe mutual funds, and more recently exchange-traded funds, are the best investment instruments for most individual investors most of the time. Many investors will want to at least experiment with owning individual stocks, and that is quite appropriate. I owned stocks for more than twenty years before I bought my first mutual fund. When people talk about "playing the market" (a term I do not like), they are usually talking about buying and selling stocks. For many it is a game, or test of skill, to pit one's own knowledge and experience against the forces of the market.

For most of us, however, we should use mutual funds or ETFs for a large portion, if not a majority of our investing. *Mutual funds* are a form of investment that pools the money of individual investors and then invests that money in selected kinds of investments. There are as many kinds of mutual funds as there are different kinds of investment products. There are stock funds, bond funds, precious metals funds, real estate funds, etc.

Table 3-1 in Chapter 3 shows some of the different categories and sub-categories for which you can buy mutual funds.

Mutual funds date from the 1920s. The Massachusetts Investment Trust Fund was first made available to investors in 1924. That fund is still operating today as part of the MFS family of mutual funds. Although available from the 1920s, funds did not become popular and widely held until about the 1960s. I bought my first mutual fund, Energy Fund, in 1969. As the name implies, it owned oil companies, utilities and other companies related to energy. It was what today we would call a sector fund, although there were not enough mutual funds in those days to represent all the sectors of the economy. I began by investing $25 a month in the fund, and after about two years, I increased that to $35 monthly. As the country was hit by the Arab oil boycott and energy crisis of the early 1970s, the fund price took a dive as did the price of most energy related stocks at that time. I continued to invest, and over time I benefitted from dollar averaging as the price of the fund fell sharply and later came back up. The fund was eventually bought by the Neuberger-Berman firm and the name was changed. Like Energy Fund, which became part of that firm's offerings, most mutual funds today are offered by large mutual fund companies that have a long list of funds available. Vanguard, Fidelity, J.P. Morgan Chase, T. Rowe Price, PIMCO and Franklin-Templeton are among the largest fund companies. These and other fund firms usually offer a wide choice of funds. They usually offer not just stock funds, but fixed income, money market and other categories of funds as well.

Fund Pros and Cons

Mutual funds have become popular with investors for several reasons. First they provide the benefits of size. By pooling the money of many investors they can make large investments and take advantage of the economies of scale. The large size reduces the per share cost of brokerage fees, research, manager expenses, etc. Funds also provide professional management. Most of us are not full time investors and do not have the time or ability to analyze potential investments in the way that full time professionals can. Hopefully the fund manager can make wise choices on behalf of the shareholders. A major advantage of funds is that they offer diversity. An individual investor may be able to own several stocks, but by buying just one share of a diversified mutual fund becomes an owner of dozens or even hundreds of individual stocks. Most funds also provide rapid liquidity. If you own an apartment house and need money from it, it may take you months to sell it. If you own a real estate mutual fund and choose to sell it, the proceeds of the sale can be in your account in twenty-four hours or less.

A significant advantage of mutual funds is that they are generally well regulated and, with a few exceptions, they have avoided major scandals. The Securities Act of 1935 required that mutual funds register with and provide detailed fund information to the Securities and Exchange Commission. The Investment Company Act of 1940 defined kinds of funds and provided additional regulatory structure for the industry. Investors can feel relatively secure that U.S. based funds are operated and managed with reasonable legal protection. Of course, there is no guarantee they will always be profitable for fund owners.

Mutual funds are not without their problems. One of the most obvious issues with funds is cost. Fund managers, office rental, advertising, research, etc. all cost money, and that must come from the revenues of the funds before any profits accrue to the shareholders. These expenses cut into fund profits, but even in bad years when there are no profits, the costs must still be paid. I discuss below what I think are reasonable expense levels for an investor to look for in choosing mutual funds.

Another problem is determining whether the fund manager's interests are aligned with those of the shareholders. A good first step in addressing this is to see if the manager is a major shareholder in the fund. If the manager isn't willing to put his or her money in the fund, why should you? Websites like www.morningstar.com and www.yahoo.com will give you information on this. Some fund companies, in order to recruit investors, will advertise that their fund managers are investors in the funds they manage. Investors can also check a fund portfolio to see if it appears to be consistent with the stated objectives of the fund. Managers are often paid on a bonus basis that may motivate them to take excessive risk in their choice of investments. You may invest in what is described as a low risk fund only to find that the manager has significantly raised the risk level. Morningstar's analysis of individual funds provides much information on the performance of fund managers, the corporate culture of fund companies, any legal or ethical issues the funds may have faced, etc. Chuck Jaffe's articles at www.marketwatch.com are a very good source of information, as is the weekly mutual fund section of *Barron's*. *Barron's* also publishes a comprehensive quarterly review of funds.

Another potential problem, especially for high income investors, is that they cannot control the income flow from funds. A shareholder may have done very well in his or her private business or profession in the current year, and be anxious to defer other income to the next year so as to reduce current year income taxes. The fund manager, however, may have attained significant capital gains for the fund that year, and the shareholder faces a tax liability that cannot be deferred. An even more difficult problem arises when a fund goes down in price in a given year even though some stock sales within the fund have generated capital gains. On paper the shareholder has a loss in fund value for that year, but may still face a tax liability for the fund's transactions. There are steps shareholders can take to reduce this problem. Index funds have low turnover and generate little in the way of tax liabilities. There are also actively managed funds, usually identified as "tax managed funds," that are designed to minimize the tax consequences of the fund. In addition, investments inside retirement, education and other tax protected accounts do not have to worry about this problem.

I will mention one other criticism of mutual funds even though I do not worry about it in my own investing, and it should not be a problem for most investors. The value of a mutual fund, based on the value of all the securities the fund owns, is calculated once a day, after the market closes. That is also the time when all the day's buy and sell orders are implemented.

This means that, if the stock market starts down at 10:00 a.m., investors cannot immediately sell shares and get out. They have to wait until settlement time after the market closes. For the investor, as opposed to the trader or speculator, this should not be a major problem.

There has been only one day I can remember, October 19, 1987, called "Black Monday," when the fact that funds are valued only once a day might have been an issue for some investors. On that day, the Dow Jones Industrial Average declined by 508 points, or 22.6%. I was watching the market carefully that day, but I did no buying or selling, so the market movement created no problem for me. In fact, in sixty years of investing, I don't think there has ever been a time when I said "Darn! I wish I could have traded that mutual fund at 11:00 a.m. instead of having to wait until after the market closed." There may be some day traders or high velocity traders who make money (or lose it!) based on the price fluctuations of a few minutes or a few hours. Most of us individual investors do not invest that way. So this is a problem I wouldn't waste much time worrying about. Considering all the pros and cons, I believe mutual funds are a good investment instrument for most of us to use in our core portfolios.

Fund Characteristics

There are several characteristics of funds with which potential buyers should be familiar. Mutual funds can be open end or closed end funds. *Open end funds* are purchased directly from the mutual fund company that sponsors the fund or through brokers representing the company. They do not trade on an exchange nor do they have a set number of shares. As investors buy the fund the company increases the number of shares available to meet the demand. If investors want to sell shares the company must buy them back. Because investors may want to sell their shares back at any time, the fund must maintain sufficient cash reserves so that it has the liquidity to meet this demand. The value of open end fund shares is determined each day after the market closes by calculating the value of all the securities owned in the fund portfolio. Most of the funds I write about in this book are open end funds.

There are also *closed end funds*. These funds have a set number of shares and they trade on an exchange much like individual stocks. When you buy shares you are buying from someone who has offered them for sale. You are not buying from a fund company. A unique characteristic of closed end funds is that the market price of shares may be above or below the net asset value of the shares. When that occurs we say it is selling at a premium or discount to its value. This cannot happen with open end funds because, as noted above, market price is the same as the net asset value. Some investors look for closed end funds selling at a discount in hopes that in the future they will profit if the fund price moves up to sell at or near net asset value. Sometimes closed end funds convert and become open end funds. If the fund is trading below net asset value at the time of the conversion, shareholders will automatically profit because the fund will trade at net asset value when it becomes open end.

Mutual funds can also be load or no-load funds. A *load* is a sales charge. A load fund can impose a charge in a number of ways. They may impose a *front end load*, which means the buyer pays a charge, perhaps 1% to as much as nearly 5%, for the privilege of buying the fund. A *back end load* is a charge levied at the time you sell the fund. Sometimes, in order to discourage rapid buying and selling, a fund will charge a back end load if the investors holds it for less than a given length of time. There are many variations funds can use in imposing loads.

It is important to remember that loads go to pay costs associated with selling the fund—commissions, advertising, sales staff, etc. Loads do not pay for fund managers, research or other items that might go to improve the performance of the fund. Then why would anyone buy a fund that imposes a sales charge? As the editor of a newsletter entitled *No-Load Portfolios,* I am probably not the most objective person on this issue. I am a strong believer that no load mutual funds are usually the best instrument for meeting the needs of the individual investor. In particular, I would urge you to beware of anyone who tries to tell you that load funds provide superior investment performance. There is no relationship whatever between loads and fund performance, and anyone telling you that is either misinformed themselves or trying to misinform you. Mutual funds must explain clearly in their advertising material and their prospectus what kinds of loads, if any, they are imposing.

There are times when it may be appropriate to own load funds. In the late 1980s I wanted to add a real estate mutual fund to my portfolio, which was mostly stock and bond funds. I had difficulty finding a real estate fund offered by a no load fund company, so for a number of years I invested regularly in a real estate fund that carried a front end load. When no load real estate funds became available, I switched my portfolio and began owning them. Also, you may use a financial planner that you like very much, and it may be that your planner is compensated by commissions rather than fees. You need to be aware that the planner is most likely to recommend funds to you that carry a load because they are the ones through which he will receive a commission. This is entirely appropriate. So long as he fully discloses to you how he is compensated, he is acting legally and in a manner consistent with the ethical standards of his profession. If you like his services and are aware of and satisfied with his method of compensation, then you have a legitimate business relationship. In my financial planning practice, I am a fee only planner, but that is a personal choice. There are good planners who have any of several reasonable compensation systems. Finally, a load becomes less important the longer you own a fund. If you pay a 4% load for a fund and then hold it for four years, it averages out to be 1% a year for those years. This is another instance in which time is the friend of the investor.

Mutual funds can be *index funds* or *actively managed funds*. Index funds are designed to replicate the performance of one of the major indexes, such as the Dow Jones Industrial Average, S&P500, Russell 2000 or the Nasdaq. Global and international funds will often use a benchmark such as the MSCI EAFE or one of the other MSCI indexes. Actively managed funds have outperforming their benchmark as a major objective. An index fund needs little active management. Because it is supposed to reflect its benchmark, a computer program can do much of the work in constructing its portfolio. An actively managed fund, which is supposed to give the investor a better return than the market, will need fund manager, research specialists, economists, etc, and thus will have higher costs than index funds. Whether actively managed funds can consistently outperform the markets is a source of much debate, and I will address that issue in Chapters 6 and 7.

One of the most important factors to consider in evaluating funds is the *expense ratio*. This is the percentage of the fund's assets spent each year on the expenses of running the fund. For example, if a fund has an expense ratio of 1.2%, that means it spends $1.20 per $100 of assets each year for the various expenses of the fund. You do not write out a check for this amount, but rather the expenses are covered by the fund, thereby reducing the return you receive as a shareholder. Index funds usually have a lower expense ratio than actively managed funds. There are some index funds with a rate of .2% or less, meaning they spend only twenty cents or less per $100 of assets on the annual expenses of running the fund. The range of expense ratios is wide. I look for index funds with a ratio of .5% or less, preferably less, and actively managed funds with a ratio of about 1.0%. There are many good funds in the 1.0%-1.5% range, and I have no problem with funds at that level. I get skeptical when the expenses exceed 1.5%, but there are sometimes reasons for the higher costs. An Asia regional fund may need to have offices and research staff in Shanghai, Hong Kong, Singapore, etc, and such costs push expense ratios higher. New, small mutual funds that do not yet have enough assets to take advantage of economies of scale will have higher expenses per share until they have had time to grow. As the total assets grow the expense ratio should come down. You can find expense ratios in several places. It will always be in the fund's prospectus and annual report, or you can find it on the mutual fund company's website. In addition, the major mutual fund websites will always have this information available.

Exchange Traded Funds

Exchange traded funds are a specific kind of mutual fund that has become very popular in the last fifteen years or so. Like closed end funds, they are traded on an exchange and can be bought and sold throughout the market day, but there are important differences between the two. For large institutional investors a major difference is that large institutions that own some of the securities in the ETF's portfolio can actually trade, or redeem, the holdings for shares of the ETF. For the individual investor ETFs can usually be counted on to trade much more closely to net asset value than closed end funds. This reduces the opportunity to profit by buying at a discount, as you sometimes can with closed end funds, but it also provides much more stability for the ETF. It gives the investor more confidence in using ETFs to meet particular needs in a portfolio.

ETFs date from 1994 when the first one was created to track the movements of the S&P500 index. For more than a decade nearly all ETFs were index funds. In more recent years the number of actively managed ETFs has grown, but they are still very much in the minority. Today there are hundreds of ETFs, and many of them are so specific in their investment objectives that they enable the investor to use them to fill very narrowly defined portfolio needs. If you want an ETF that invests only in the small cap stocks of a specific emerging country in Asia or Africa, you can probably find one. On the other hand, if you want a broadly based fund that tracks the total market of the United States, Europe or even the world, those are available also.

A major advantage of ETFs is that they have very low expense ratios. Many have expense ratios of .3% or less, and even actively managed ETFs have much lower ratios than their traditional mutual fund counterparts. The emergence of ETFs has had the additional advantage of pressuring traditional open end mutual funds to keep their ratios low as well. It is clear that some of the large mutual fund companies have lowered the expense ratios of their index funds because of the competition from ETFs.

Choosing Your Mutual Funds

If you have not owned mutual funds before, it is very easy to get started building a mutual fund portfolio. You may have a financial planner or investment counselor to help you, and that's fine, but you can easily do it yourself if you prefer. First, familiarize yourself with the general subject of mutual funds. You may want to read one or two good books on the subject. A good place to start would be John Bogle's *Common Sense on Mutual Funds* (2009). There is even a *Mutual Funds for Dummies* (2011), which would probably be inappropriate for any readers of this book! There are always new books coming out. You can also look at the mutual fund sections of the major financial websites. The websites of the major mutual fund companies— American Century, Fidelity, T. Rowe Price, Vanguard, etc.—can be very helpful.

Second, you need to decide on your investment objectives. What is the goal of the portfolio? If you are forty years old and are investing to retire, perhaps in a 401k, you can pick mutual funds some of which carry fairly high risk. You can also develop an asset allocation plan with most of your money, perhaps 70%-80%, going into stock funds. You will also need to decide where bond funds, real estate funds and other asset categories fit into your plan. As you get older, you will want to let your portfolio become more conservative. If you are a fifty year old planning for retirement, or a parent with a child entering college in ten years, your investment allocations will be different.

Third, you will need to choose the mutual funds that best meet your objectives. You should feel free to look at both traditional mutual funds and ETFs. Both are good, and you may find as you build your portfolio that you will want some of each in your holdings. There is plenty of help available to you. Magazines like *Kiplinger's* and *Forbes* regularly publish lists of their favorite funds. Websites like www.morningstar.com and www.marketwatch.com do the same. Many websites also provide screening tools that enable you to input a set of characteristics you are looking for in funds. The screen will then provide you a list of funds that meet your criteria.

In considering fund objectives, you should look at the fund's prospectus. This is an official document written by attorneys in "legalese," and you do not need to try to read and understand all of it. Nevertheless, it does provide important information about the fund. In particular, it will describe the official investment objectives of the fund, the ones the managers are expected to abide by in selecting securities to go in the fund's portfolio. This will help you decide if the fund is right for you. The prospectus will also include an explanation of the fund's expenses and information on past performance. If you are an attorney you may want to read the document in more detail. It will provide information on the fund company, managers, risks, etc. Not being an attorney, I find the descriptions of the fund's objectives and expenses to be the most helpful parts of the prospectus. You would never want this document to be your only source of information before buying a mutual fund.

I hesitate to recommend television as a source of serious financial information, but there are programs that can be helpful so long as you remember that most of the guests you see interviewed want to sell you something. CNBC is the most widely viewed of the financial networks. Its programs vary greatly, from Jim Cramer's shouting to Larry Kudlow's political opinions, but there is also a lot of good, solid information presented, including even that on Cramer's and Kudlow's programs. In many broker's offices you will find the TV tuned to CNBC throughout the day, but with the volume muted. They can glance at the screen and check the market numbers occasionally, and bring up the volume if they see something that looks like it might be interesting. Bloomberg News and Fox Business News are also good sources, and on public television, *Nightly Business Report,* which is on Monday through Friday, is a good source for getting a succinct presentation of the day's market and economic news.

Part of choosing your mutual funds is to decide how many you want to own. As noted in Chapter 3, you may own as few as two or three funds, and you can certainly have a diversified portfolio with no more than five to seven funds. If you want to own more you need to be sure you have the time and interest to continually monitor and evaluate all the funds. I cannot think of many reasons why even the most sophisticated investor would want to own more than twelve to fifteen funds, and it is hard to justify even that number unless there are very special circumstances. One lesson I have learned over the years is that it is easy to "accumulate" funds without much rhyme or reason. You look at your portfolio one day and say, "Why did I ever buy that fund?" You are better off knowing why you own each of the funds you have and how they fit into your overall portfolio strategy.

Fourth, after you have decided on the funds you want to own, you are ready to implement your plan. If you are buying ETFs or closed end funds, you will get them through your broker, or if you trade on line, you can make your purchases directly. If you are buying traditional mutual funds, you can buy them from the fund company, or in many cases you can buy them through brokers, including internet brokers with whom the fund company has made an arrangement to make their funds available. I would suggest you ease your money into your portfolio over time even if you have a large cash balance (maybe Uncle Ed gave you $50,000) available for investment. You might invest monthly, every other month or even quarterly.

This helps you avoid investing too much of your money at one time, possibly at elevated prices, and enables you to take advantage of dollar averaging. Sometimes you may have to invest more at first to meet the minimum purchase requirement of a fund, but after that initial investment, future purchases can be adjusted to your individual needs.

Finally, you should monitor your portfolio but not micromanage it. You will want to review your asset allocations regularly, probably annually, as discussed in Chapter 3. If your portfolio is out of balance with your investment goals, you can sell or buy fund shares as needed to bring your portfolio back into line. Occasionally you may want to substitute a new fund for an existing one. Perhaps a respected fund manager has left the fund and you do not feel confident about the new one. A fund might be involved in "mission creep," i.e. not investing in accordance with the fund's stated objectives, which is why you bought the fund in the first place. What you do not want to do is chase performance, or yield. Some funds will always do better at some times than others. If you have chosen a good set of funds, you do not want to be constantly selling some fund to buy another because the new one had surprisingly good performance last quarter.

Buying and Selling Financial Products

Financial products are traded in different ways. No-load mutual funds are usually bought and sold directly from the mutual fund firm that sponsors them. Large companies such as American Century, Fidelity, Oakmark, T. Rowe Price and Vanguard have 800 numbers and websites, and you can buy or sell funds at no cost by contacting them through their phone or internet. You should not expect financial planners or brokers to offer you much help in your decisions because as the term, "no-load" implies, there is no sales charge or commission to compensate these people. Financial professionals will help you buy load funds, and because they are compensated, they can also provide information and advice to help you with your investment decisions. Exchange traded funds, as the name indicates, trade on regular stock exchanges in a manner similar to the trading of stocks and bonds.

If you want to be an active investor in exchange traded funds, stocks, municipal bonds, corporate bonds and similar products, you will need to have an account with a broker. This can be a full service "bricks and mortar" office or a discount broker with whom you communicate mainly through the internet. Full service brokers can help you with investment decisions, portfolio building, establishment of retirement accounts and other financial matters. Discount brokers provide you with the opportunity to trade for your account through their website, but they are limited in amount of advice and counsel they can give. According, fees and charges will be higher with the full service broker. If all you are doing is buying or selling stocks or funds, the discount brokers' commissions are quite low, often $10 or less per transaction. Some financial companies, including Vanguard, Schwab and Fidelity, now offer their own exchange traded funds, and they enable you to trade ETFs at little or no cost so long as you are trading the funds they sponsor. You can buy U.S. Treasury notes, bills and bonds, including savings bonds, directly from the government at www.treasurydirect.gov.

Mutual Funds and Other Investments

While mutual funds and exchange traded funds are a good choice for most investors, and it is possible to build a profitable portfolio using nothing but such funds, it is also appropriate to include them with other types of securities in a diversified portfolio. You might build the basic portion of your holdings with traditional funds and ETFs, but also include some individual stocks, bonds, commodities, etc. in your investments. We address this subject in the next three chapters.

Chapter 6
Are Markets Efficient? Is the Walk Random? And Do We Care?

The debate over the nature of stock market movements began just about the time I made my first stock market investment in August 1952. Of course, I was totally unaware of it and would not have understood it if I had known about it. It was at that time, the early 1950s, that a group of scholars, primarily at the University of Chicago, began to explore the question of how stock market movements could be studied using rigorous research techniques. I will address the various aspects of that academic discussion in this chapter. In the following chapters, I will discuss how individual investors can take that information and use it in a practical way in building and managing their portfolios.

Markowitz and Modern Portfolio Theory

One of the most important research papers to emerge from that era was a doctoral dissertation written by Harry Markowitz on the subject of asset allocation. It was one of the earliest attempts to address that issue in a systematic way, and Markowitz made the case that a portfolio including non-correlating assets will carry less risk than the risk of each individual security in the portfolio. Markowitz turned the attention of scholars from the risk of individual holdings to the risk of the portfolio as a whole. That idea seems amazingly simple today, but it was a major innovation at the time. He also focused attention on the relationship between risk and return, something we take for granted today but not then. His paper was published as a book, *Portfolio Selection,* in 1952, and became a must read for those in the investment field. Years later this work was instrumental in his sharing in the Nobel Prize for Economics in 1990.

The set of ideas explored by Markowitz, along with a number of other scholars of the day, came to be known as *Modern Portfolio Theory (MPT)*. This includes asset allocation, individual security risk, total portfolio risk, correlation of individual stocks with the total market, etc. If you want to apply some of his wisdom to your portfolio, you might explore the website, www.guidedchoice.com. This comes from an advisory firm that he helped establish, primarily to provide advice on 401k's. The site enables you to input information on your income, assets, age, etc. and helps you estimate what kind of income you can expect in retirement.

Fama and Efficient Markets

Eugene Fama was another of the early students of stock market movements whose work has greatly influenced most of us who are investors whether we realize it or not. He also ignited one of the great debates that market scholars and practitioners have engaged in for over half a century, with his development of the *efficient market hypothesis* (EMH). This hypothesis states that, because the market quickly responds to all available public information, stocks will be correctly valued most of the time. It suggests that new information is quickly absorbed by the market, and stock prices will almost immediately adjust based on the new information. While Fama stated his case clearly and firmly, he was not the first researcher to look at the question of market efficiency. As early as 1900, a French mathematician by the name of Louis Bachelier was doing research that suggested both market efficiency and market unpredictability. In the 1930s, economists working with the Cowles Commission for Research in Economics came to similar conclusions.

The reason the efficient market hypothesis has been so controversial, of course, is because of its implication that markets follow no pattern and future market movements cannot be predicted. To some degree the debate broke down along professional lines of academic versus practitioner. The academics believed that most objective research supports the idea of an efficient market. The late Paul Samuelson, a prominent member of the Harvard faculty, and Burt Malkiel of Princeton, were among the strong supporters of this position. Many practitioners took the other position. They argued that, by analyzing such corporate data as earnings reports, price/earnings ratios, book value, cash flow and other financial and economic data, they can make informed projections about future price movements. Others, those called chartists, claimed they could create charts with past price movement patterns, and this would enable them to predict future price patterns. Critics come down especially hard on the chartists. They say that past price movements predict future price movements with the same predictability that past coin flips predict future ones. If you are flipping a coin and it comes up heads thirty times in a row, the chances of it coming up heads on the thirty-first flip are still 50/50. They would say the same is true of stock market patterns. Past up/down stock price movements, they contend, tell you little about future price movements.

While it is not entirely fair to question the motives of practitioners, it can be noted that they have a certain vested interest in creating doubt about the efficient market hypothesis. After all, the brokers, financial planners, pension fund managers, mutual fund managers and other financial professionals are supposed to be able to pick stocks that will increase in price in the future. They claim to have superior knowledge to individual investors, and they want to sell their services and their funds to those investors. If markets are efficient that raises questions as to whether they have anything to sell.

Advocates of the efficient market hypotheses (EMH) seemed to get the better of the argument for about the first twenty years after Fama first introduced the concept. After that a series of events occurred that brought increased skepticism and questioning to the issue. One such event was Black Monday, October 19, 1987, when the Dow Jones Industrial Average fell 508 points, or 22.6%, in a single day. A little more than a decade later, the market suffered from the collapse of technology stocks that took the market down 37.8% from January 2000 to March 2002. Then in 2007-09 the market responded to the real estate crisis with a drop of 53.8%. How can markets get so far from their intrinsic value, EMH critics could ask, that it takes market adjustments of this magnitude to bring them back in line. If EMH advocates argue that market efficiency will bring stock prices back in line in the long run, skeptics will ask just how long is the long run.

Perhaps the most serious questions about EMH came from within the academic community itself. In the last quarter of the twentieth century, a new academic area of study emerged, combining aspects of both economics and finance. It was called *be-*

havioral finance. A major representative of this new field was Robert Shiller, a professor at Yale who was well known among academics and became familiar to the general public as well with the publication of his book, *Irrational Exuberance,* in 2000. In that book he argued that investors can be very irrational at times and he suggested that at that time stocks were very overvalued. It was only months later that the collapse of the high tech stocks began. Behavioral finance scholars argue that investors are often not rational and make decisions that have little to do with economic reality.

One example of this that I can relate to, and I expect many investors can as well, is the investor who buys a stock only to see it decline sharply in price. He becomes disillusioned with the stock and wants to get rid of it, but he wants to wait to sell it until it gets back to the price he paid for it. There is nothing rational about such a strategy. If the stock is now a bad investment, what the investor originally paid for it is irrelevant. Somehow he feels better if the stock gets back to its original purchase price before he sells it, but that has little to do with rational investing or efficient markets.

Some interesting arguments questioning the unpredictability of the market are presented in the annual publication, *Stock Trader's Almanac,* edited by Jeffrey A. Hirsch and Yale Hirsch. This is a first rate publication that I read regularly and use as a reference in gathering data for our newsletter. The *Almanac* provides information on at least three market patterns that appear to challenge the idea that markets are random and unpredictable. The first is the "January Effect" that says that the direction of the stock market in January is a good indicator of the direction of the market for the entire year. The second is the "Sell in May and Go Away" theory that shows that most market profits come between November and May. Third is the "Presidential Cycle" theory that contends the market does better in the final two years of a presidential administration than in the first two years. The idea here is that presidents, wanting to get reelected, will make their hard decisions, such as to raise taxes or cut popular programs, early in their administration, leading to poorer market results in those first years. These patterns occur with sufficient regularity, the *Almanac* contends, as to call the EMH into question.

I have no quarrel with these three market patterns, but I would suggest that only the "sell in May and go away" theory is likely to be of help in actually managing a portfolio. I can see the logic of buying an index fund around November 1, holding it until May, selling it and putting the proceeds into a money market fund until the following November, and then starting the process all over again. I think it would be more difficult to devise a practical buy/sell strategy based on the other two trends.

Fama's views have evolved over time, based on his own research and that of others. He later rejected the most pure and doctrinaire views of EMH. As his views on EMH changed, one of his critics said the Pope had declared God is dead. I think it would be more appropriate to just suggest that the Pope has changed his view of God somewhat. Part of the debate depends on how one defines the word, "efficient." How many anomalies, or exceptions to the rule, can there be, and how long can they last, and still call markets efficient?

Markowitz and Fama were not the only scholars to address such issues as asset allocation, efficient markets, portfolio risk and other aspects of market behavior. Other prominent names would include Fischer Black, Paul Samuelson, Myron Scholes, Franco Modigliani and Merton Miller among others. If you want to pursue these subjects further, check the writings of any of these. The research scholarship that began at the University of Chicago also spread to other campuses, including MIT, Harvard, Princeton and the Wharton School at the University of Pennsylvania. On the west coast outstanding finance programs developed at Stanford and the University of California-Berkeley. Today there is significant research going on not just at the "big name" campuses but at universities and colleges throughout the nation.

Malkiel's Random Walk

While he is very much a part of the academic community, Burton Malkiel deserves credit for taking academic concepts beyond the ivy walls of academe and presenting them in clear and easy-to-understand language to the general investing public. His 1973 book, *A Random Walk Down Wall Street,* became a classic for the investing world. I read the book a few years after it was published, and it changed my investing thinking in fundamental ways. Among the investment lessons I have learned over the years, many of them came from Malkiel. He has had an illustrious career. He has an M.B.A. from Harvard and a Ph.D. from Princeton. Prior to joining the Princeton faculty he served on the President's Council of Economic Advisors and as Dean of the Yale School of Management. He has also worked in the investment industry, including serving on the board of Vanguard.

Malkiel is best known, however, for his career at Princeton, his book and his strong advocacy of investing in index funds. As the title of his book indicates, he has made the public familiar with the term, *random walk.* He says that markets move randomly, are unpredictable, and past stock price movements provide no information that will enable investors to predict future movements or outperform a buy-and-hold strategy.

With a basic investment strategy that is clear and easy to understand, Malkiel recommends owning a portfolio of widely

81

diversified no-load index funds with low expense ratios. To get the wide diversification he wants he would reach beyond just the Dow Jones Industrial Average and the S&P500 indexes. In terms of what is available today, I expect he would use funds such as the Vanguard Total Stock Market Index Fund (VTSMX), the Vanguard Total Stock Market ETF (VTI), the Fidelity Spartan Total Market Index Fund (FSTMX) or the SPDR Dow Jones Total Market ETF (TMV). Note: these are my recommendations, not Prof. Malkiel's. These funds attempt to achieve the performance of the entire universe of U.S. publicly traded stocks, not just the largest ones.

Malkiel consistently points out the importance of keeping costs as low as possible, and points out that buying index funds is the best way to achieve this. Even among index funds expense ratios can vary. As of late 2011 the expense ratios of the funds mentioned above were: VTI (.07%), FSTMX (.10%), VTSMX (.17%) and TMV (.20%). Finally, he recommends regular, periodic investing so as to take advantage of dollar cost averaging.

Bogle's Index Funds

If Burt Malkiel introduced the random walk theory to the public, John Bogle created the index funds that enabled them to implement an investment strategy based on that theory using index funds as their investment vehicle. Bogle was born in 1929 and spent his entire career in the mutual fund business. In his college years at Princeton, he wrote his senior thesis on "The Economic Role of the Investment Company." Bogle criticized mutual fund companies for emphasizing marketing rather than service, and urged investors to make low costs a major factor in their choice of mutual funds. In 1996, at the age of 67, he had a heart transplant, but it did not stop him from continuing his professional career and active lifestyle. Just three years later, in

1999, he published his book, *Common Sense On Mutual Funds,* which became a best seller. Ten years later, in 2009, a tenth anniversary edition of the book with much new material, was published. John Bogle's name is forever associated with the Vanguard firm and index funds.

He was a founder of Vanguard in 1974, and the company opened its first index fund a year later. In 1976, they offered the First Index Investment Trust, a fund designed to reflect the performance of the S&P500 index. Four years later it was renamed the Vanguard 500 Index Fund, and it remains today one of the largest of all mutual funds. The economist, Paul Samuelson, was an early enthusiastic supporter of index funds. He said his index funds put his six children through college. Still active when he was 91, he declared in a speech in Boston that the creation of the index fund was equivalent to the invention of the wheel or the alphabet (Bogle, *Don't Count,* p. 396).

Since the 500 fund reflected the market of only the largest 500 companies, the company in 1989 created the Extended Market Fund, which tracked the performance of all the other publicly traded companies, about 5000 at that time. In 1986 they offered the Vanguard Total Bond Index Fund to give investors a chance to allocate some of their money to the fixed income side of the market. The 1990s saw additional expansion, as the company offered mid-cap, international, value and growth index funds. The company entered the ETF market in 2001 with the offering of extended market and total stock market ETFs.

Bogle has established a reputation as a champion of the small investor, who is the primary consumer of the mutual fund business. In his book, *Don't Count on It* (2011), he addresses such issues as shortcomings in our capitalist system, abuses in the mutual fund business and the need for true entrepreneurship and innovation. There are some areas in which it dissents somewhat from others with similar investing ideas. He is not an enthusiast about regular rebalancing. He is not against rebalancing, but he just does not believe it significantly enhances investment performance, a point with which I would disagree. He also used to have little interest in international investing. He argued that the largest U.S. companies did so much business overseas that they provided all the international diversification an investor needed. More recently he has softened his views on this and has suggested that index portfolios should include funds that provide international diversification.

Bogle's fundamental philosophy of investing is that investors should expect to get their share of the market's return over time. If the long term return of the stock market is 9%, then investors should expect a broadly diversified index portfolio to provide them with a return of 9% less investment costs. Bogle would contend that those who promise to provide you with a greater return than the general market provides, based on their superior knowledge of investing and the markets, are unlikely to be able to follow through on their promise. Many writers have attempted to explain his views, but he put it very succinctly himself when he wrote "...own the entire U.S. market, own it at very low cost, and hang on to it forever" (*Don't Count,* p. 388). Today he might say the entire market rather than just the U.S. market, but in a nutshell that is John Bogle.

If You Want More

If you would like to explore further the issues of modern portfolio theory, asset allocation, efficient markets, random walk and similar issues there is plenty for you to look at. One of the most thorough of recent books supporting the Malkiel/Bogle position is Richard A. Ferri's *The Power of Pas-*

sive Investing (2011), in which Bogle wrote the foreword. Two books that are more critical of this position are *The Myth of the Rational Market* (2009), by Justin Fox and *Far From Random* (2009) by Richard Lehman. Lehman challenges the idea of the unpredictability of the market and presents his own strategy for predicting it. It is what he calls "trend channel analysis," and serious students of the subject ought to take a look at it.

One of my favorite books, one that is easy to read and easy to understand is *The Gone Fishin' Portfolio* (2008), by Alexander Green. Another very readable book is Allan Roth's *How a Second Grader Beats Wall Street* (2009). Both of these books are supporters of the views of Malkiel and Bogle. If you want to get your children (or anyone else) interested in investing, either of these books would make a good Christmas or birthday present.

Efficient Markets and Random Walks: My View

I have spent a lot of time reading and thinking about these issues through the years. They have influenced my investing, and my views have evolved over time. The efficient market hypothesis has been intensely debated in the popular press, in the pages of academic journals, at numerous financial conferences and seminars and between academics and practitioners. I have come to believe that efficient markets are best described not by an either/or answer but as points on a continuum. At one extreme I would suggest that many markets are highly, if not perfectly, efficient. There is a steady and massive flow of information about large-cap stocks that trade on the major exchanges of North America and Europe. In spite of events like Black Monday or the real estate crisis, these markets seem to me to have a high level of efficiency. At the other extreme I would suggest that the small-cap markets of emerging economies, perhaps Viet Nam and South Africa, would be much less efficient. Other world markets would fit somewhere along the continuum.

I am less concerned about the theoretical question of whether markets are efficient than I am in the more specific issues related to the random walk. While I am tentative in my thinking about efficient markets, I am much more convinced by the arguments made by Burton Malkiel and John Bogle. The evidence supporting random walk and the use of index funds is overwhelming, and I do most of my investing based on those concepts. I will address those issues in the next two chapters.

Chapter 7
Your Foundation Portfolio:
Simple, Disciplined, Boring and Profitable

A good investment should begin with a foundation portfolio that, as the title suggests, should be simple, disciplined, boring and profitable. It should be simple in the sense that it consists of a relatively few broadly diversified index funds that are traded infrequently, usually at the time of annual rebalancing. It should be boring because there is nothing exciting about watching a portfolio of just a few index funds that are bought and sold infrequently. There is no need to check the market every hour or every day in order to buy or sell based on signals from some technical chart, computer program or the comments of a talking head on cable television. The late Paul Samuelson has been quoted as saying, "Investing should be like watching paint dry. If you want excitement, take $800 and go to Las Vegas." Personal note: If you want excitement, I would be glad to have you come to my home town of Las Vegas, but Samuelson made that statement a number of years ago. If you are coming today, I suggest you bring more than $800.

Your portfolio should be disciplined because it is implemented by following a few simple steps. You will need to establish an asset allocation plan and adhere to it even when the temptation is to do otherwise. Annual rebalancing requires discipline because it is almost always counter-intuitive. It usually requires that you sell winners and buy losers in order to bring your portfolio back into line with your asset allocation goals. That is hard to explain and brag about at the neighborhood cocktail party.

A Foundation Portfolio: How Much? How Large?

When I first started investing in 1952 my portfolio was all stocks (just two) and a few U.S. savings bonds. It was also what you would call actively managed. I watched the stocks on a regular basis. As time passed and I read Malkiel's *Random Walk* and other books on index funds and passive investing, I gradually shifted more of my assets to mutual funds, especially index funds. That eventually evolved into a policy of having two different portfolios, a foundation portfolio and an actively managed portfolio.

How much of your portfolio should be in each? As with many aspects of investing, there are no hard and fast rules. Burt Malkiel is a name synonymous with passive investing, but I have heard him say in lectures that he enjoys trying to pick individual stocks and holds some of his assets in an actively managed portfolio. He has suggested that he holds about 80% of his investments in a passively managed portfolio. Dick Davis, the legendary market analyst, founder of *Dick Davis Digest* (which I have had the privilege of contributing to) and author of *The Dick David Dividend* (2008), also advocates an 80/20 division. He says very firmly and persuasively, "I've come to the unequivocal conclusion that most of the money of most investors should be in index funds" (Davis, 256). Without identifying a specific number, William F. Sharpe, 1990 Nobel Prize winner and developer of the Sharpe ratio, says that "most" of his investments are in index funds.

I believe the 80/20 division is a reasonable breakdown for most investors. If you prefer a 70% or 75% commitment to passive investing, that is fine. Even starting with just two-thirds in passive investing can work. If you want less than that in your passive portfolio, you probably are not yet convinced by the literature on passive investing. I would suggest you keep reading the research on the subject and keep experimenting with your own investing. You will eventually decide what is right for you. I think the 80/20 split works for me, but I also think it makes sense to address the subject in a different way. I suggest the following:

> The portion of your portfolio devoted to active investing should be no more than the amount you can afford to lose without it affecting your lifestyle.

If some of the money in your actively managed portfolio is money that, if lost, would cause you to have to postpone remodeling the house, taking your spouse on a cruise or paying your son or daughter's tuition, then that money should not be actively managed. If you have $10 million to invest, I would not necessarily suggest that you put 80% of it in a passive portfolio. In that case you could probably lose half of your assets or more without it affecting your lifestyle. The 80/20 division is a good guideline, but it is just that, a guideline.

Why the Winners Equal Less Than the Losers

In most situations the number of winners equals the number of losers. In a tennis tournament the number of games players win will exactly equal the number of games players lose. At the end of the NFL football season teams will have won the same number of games as teams have lost. Only in a fantasy world can nearly everyone be winners. On the radio show, "Prairie Home Companion," Garrison Keeler likes to talk about his mythical community, Lake Wobegon, "where all the women are beautiful and all the children are above average." Alas, in the real world not all of the children can be above average, and in the real world of finance the gains of investors cannot equal more than the losses of investors.

Unfortunately, in the world of finance it is even slightly worse than that. Unlike the sports world where games won equal games lost, there is an additional negative factor in the financial markets. Over a given period of time stock market profits will equal slightly less than stock market losses. The reason for this is *transaction costs,* all those costs that go into making the market function, including brokerage fees, mutual fund salaries, office expenses, advertising costs, etc. This is why, throughout this book, I have emphasized that the expense ratio is one of the most important considerations in choosing a mutual fund.

The Outperformance of Passive Investments

The consistent outperformance of passively managed index funds over actively managed funds is the main reason prominent investors such as those mentioned above recommend that as much as 80% of one's portfolio be invested in passive funds. Study after study, research project after research project, show that they consistently outperform actively managed funds. It is important to remember that the real question is not active v. passive management, or index funds v. other funds. The crucial factor to consider is the cost of running the fund. The expense ratio is one of the most important things to know about a fund.

Others would include the fund's objectives, the experience and background of the fund manager and the fund's multi-year performance. Of all these factors, however, the expense ratio is the one that is most likely to predict the future performance of the fund. Expense ratios relate to passive and active management in that passively managed index funds are likely to be among the funds with the lowest expenses. That is not always the case. There are actively managed funds with very low expense ratios, but in general passively managed funds will be the ones with the lowest operating costs, and that cost advantage is reflected in their performance record.

There are numerous studies that address this subject. Richard Ferri points to a study by Lipper, the financial research firm, which focuses on the first index fund, the Vanguard 500 Index Fund (Ferri, p.37). Lipper looked at the 25 year period, 1985-2009, and compared the Vanguard 500 Index Fund with the 136 domestic equity funds that existed throughout that time frame and used the S&P500 index as a benchmark. Lipper found that over the 25 year period, the Vanguard fund had a better performance record than 66% of the actively managed funds.

One response to this would be to just invest in one of the 34% of actively managed funds that outperformed the index. Easier said than done! There are two problems here. One is that no one knows ahead of time which funds will have superior performance, and even more important, the fact that a fund does well in one period is no indicator that it will do well in the future. David Solin makes this point using a study by Professor Edward S. O'Neal. O'Neal studied the performance of 495 actively managed funds that had the stated objective of outperforming the S&P500 index (Solin, 2006, p.39-40). In the five year period of July 1993 through June 1998, only 46% of the funds did as well as the index. He then repeated the study for the next five years, 1998-2003. In the second five-year period only 8% of the funds outperformed the index. More importantly, only 2% of the funds beat the S&P500 in both of the five-year time periods. This shows the difficulty of choosing funds that will do well in the future by looking at past performance.

Allan Roth looks at the problem from a different perspective (Roth, p. 97-98). He examined the effect of owning multiple mutual funds. Most of us do not own just one mutual fund. We own several. Using Monte Carlo simulation Roth studied the likelihood of a portfolio of actively managed funds outperforming a U.S. total stock market index fund over a one-year period of time. His results show the following:

Number of Actively Managed Funds Owned	Likelihood of Outperforming Total Market Index Fund
1 fund	42%
5 funds	32%
10 funds	25%

This suggests the more actively managed mutual funds you own, the lower the chances of your portfolio outperforming a total market index fund. His study also showed your chances to be even lower, the longer you owned the portfolio. For example, for a ten fund portfolio, the chances fell to 9% over five years, 6% over ten years and 1% over twenty-five years.

The argument is sometimes made that actively managed funds should be able to outperform index funds in bear markets. After all, when the stock market is falling, index funds should, by definition, fall an equal amount. This is when active managers should be able to protect their investors. They can sell stocks in their portfolio, hold cash and wait for the next recovery. Unfortunately, the facts do not bear this out. The Schwab Center for Investment Research (keep in mind that Schwab sponsors both index and actively managed funds) studied 120 index funds and 2,100 actively managed funds over a fifteen year period, 1986-2001. Their conclusions:

> Index funds outperform actively managed funds in 55% of down markets
> In market declines of 10% or more, index funds outperform 75% of the time
> In the longest market declines, those of five consecutive months or longer, index funds outperform 100% of the time

Perhaps the most comprehensive study does not focus on active or passive management at all. Morningstar undertook a study that looked at two factors: (1) Morningstar's own five-star evaluation system; and (2) the expense ratios of the funds. It studied mutual funds in five categories: domestic equity, international equity, balanced, taxable bond and municipal bond. It then examined each of the five categories by looking at the five-star funds (the highest rating) and the one-star funds (the lowest rating). To look at expenses it ranked the funds in each category from highest expense ratios to lowest expense ratios. It divided the list into quintiles and studied those in the highest and lowest quintiles. Morningstar has an interest in studying the effectiveness of its star rating system, and I assume the firm would like to be able to state that the system is the best available predictor of future fund performance. Morningstar analyst Russell Kinnel, writing on the firm's website ("Fund Spy," August 9, 2010), commented on the study as follows:

> If there's anything in the whole world of mutual funds that you can take to the bank, it's that expense ratios help you make a better decision. In

every single time period and data point tested, low-cost funds beat high-cost ones.

Expense ratios are strong predictors of performance. In every asset class over every time period, the cheapest quintile produced higher total returns than the most expensive quintile. For example, the cheapest quintile in 2005 in domestic equity returned an annualized 3.35% versus 2.02% for the most expensive quintile over the ensuing five years.

Investors should make expense ratios a primary test for fund selection. They are still the most dependable predictor of performance.

On the question of which is the better predictor, stars or expense ratios, both did well. Expense ratios did slightly better, being better predictors than the stars in 23 of 40 categories studied (58%). In virtually every category—all six fund types and all time frames—five-star funds outperformed one-star funds and the lowest quintile expense ratios outperformed the highest quintile expense ratios. Quite appropriately, the study concludes with a reminder that even these two factors, stars and expenses, are not sufficient for making a decision to buy a mutual fund. You need to also consider the manager, strategy, stewardship and other fund characteristics in determining which funds are right for your portfolio.

All Index Funds Are Not Created Equal

There are a variety of kinds of index funds. The most common type, and the type I recommend for most foundation portfolios, are called cap-weighted index funds. This means that the companies with a large capitalization (the total value of their publicly traded shares) have more influence on the index than smaller companies. For example, in the S&P500 index companies such as Apple, Exxon and General Electric will have much more impact on the movement of the index than the smaller companies in the index. There have been times when 70%-75% of the stocks in the index fell in price, but the largest companies rose, causing the total index to go up. Because the historic S&P500 index, with which we are most familiar, is cap-weighted, most of the funds that use that index as a benchmark are also cap-weighted. The Vanguard 500 Index Fund (VPINX) and the Fidelity Spartan 500 Index Fund (FUSEX) would be examples of such funds. The SPDR 500 Index (SPY) and the iShares 500 Index (IVV) are exchange-traded funds that alsofit this category.

There are also *equal-weighted index funds*, where each company included has about the same impact on the movement of the index. The Rydex 500 Equal Weight Index Fund (RSP) is an example. As you would expect, when large cap stocks are outperforming other stocks, the traditional cap-weighted index funds will outperform the others. If mid-cap or small-cap stocks are outperforming larger companies, then the equal-weighted funds will be the better performers. Since no one can predict which companies will do the best over any given period of time, it is impossible to know which funds will be the best to own over that period.

There is no limit to the number of variations fund companies can use to create new types of mutual funds. There are funds that are designed to provide some multiple of an index's return. For example, a 2X S&P fund attempts to double the performance (either up or down) of the index. A 3X funds wants to triple the performance, etc. There are inverse, or short, funds where the objective it is to move in the opposite direction of the index. A Dow inverse index fund would be expected to decline by 15% if the Dow index increases by 15%. There are also 2X, 3X, etc. inverse funds. A 2X S&P500 inverse index fund would be expected to increase by 20% if the S&P500 index declines by 10%. To find examples of these kinds of funds, look at the fund offerings of the Rydex and Pro Fund companies.. Both have a comprehensive list of such funds.

Funds such as these may have a role in an actively managed portfolio. If used at all, they need to be part of a carefully thought out strategy. In constructing a foundation portfolio, I recommend that investors stick with the basic "plain vanilla" cap-weighted index funds.

Building Your Foundation Portfolio

Your portfolio needs to be comprehensive enough to include most of the major investment categories, including some investments that have low correlation with others. Chapter 3 provides examples of different kinds of portfolios. The simplest portfolio could be:

U.S. total stock market fund	40%
U.S. total bond market fund	40%
International stock market fund	20%

If you want to make your portfolio a little more comprehensive, you can take the 40% in the total stock market fund and replace it with two other funds, 30% in an S&P500 index fund and 10% in an extended market fund, which covers those stocks not included in the S&P500. You might split the 20% in the international fund, and invest it 10% in a developed markets fund and 10% in an emerging markets fund. The bond portion of the portfolio could be divided between short-term and long-term bond funds or between corporate and government bond funds. If you want to keep 5% in cash, I suggest you do so by peeling it off from the 40% bond allocation.

You could broaden your portfolio a bit by adding such categories as real estate, commodities, precious metals or foreign currencies. I do not necessarily advocate adding these, but they are available to you. I think it is important that you keep the portfolio simple enough to be easy to understand, monitor and manage.

You can keep your foundation portfolio simple by having contributions to it be automatic. If your portfolio is part of a 401k, 403b or similar account, you can have your contributions go directly from your employer to your portfolio. Otherwise, you can authorize your broker or mutual fund company to automatically withdraw a specific amount each month or quarter from your bank account and have it invested in your portfolio as you direct.

The investments you designate as your foundation portfolio may be located in several different places. Some may be inside tax protected accounts, and some may not. There are no hard and fast rules, but generally you will want your investments that create current income, like bonds and dividend paying stocks or funds, to be inside 401k's, individual retirement accounts and other tax protected accounts when possible.

As I have already indicated, a critically important step in managing your foundation portfolio is your annual rebalancing. You can rebalance by selling some of your winners and buying your losers to bring them back into line with your asset allocation targets. If you are fortunate enough to have extra money available at rebalancing time, you can just add the money to those categories that have fallen below the target allocations.

Other than your regular periodic investing, your rebalancing should be the major buy/sell activity in your foundation portfolio. Your trading, individual stock selection and aggressive investing should take place in your actively managed portfolio, to which we will turn in the next chapter.

Applying 80/20 to Portfolio Management

Earlier in the chapter I mentioned the names of several well-known investors who invest 80% of their money in a foundation portfolio and 20% in actively managed securities. The 80/20 principle can be applied more generally. You have probably heard people refer to the 80/20 principle in business. Employers may tell you that 20% of their employees cause 80% of their problems. Store managers may say that 20% of the customers register 80% of the complaints. I would suggest that the 80/20 principle can be applied to portfolio management as well..

It may be that you have little interest in investing. You do what you have to in order to provide for a secure retirement and to meet lifetime needs such as home purchase, college expenses, international travel, etc. Beyond that, however, you have little interest in, and get little satisfaction from, overseeing your investments, choosing the right stocks to buy and managing your portfolio. In that case, I would suggest you put all your investment money, not just 80%, in your foundation portfolio. Spend the minimum amount of time necessary for monitoring your passively managed index portfolio, and then spend the rest of your time on those things you really enjoy.

Some writers suggest you can manage your portfolio in amazingly small amounts of time. Dan Solin, in his *Smart Investing* book, suggests that you can do most of what you need to do in overseeing a passively managed portfolio in about ninety minutes a year (Solin, *Smart Investing,* p. 6). In his

401k book, he says the most important policy decision for a portfolio, setting asset allocation targets, can be made in about fifteen minutes a year (Solin, *Smartest 401k Book*, p. 37). Alexander Green, in his *Gone Fishin'* book, describes his system and says, "Best of all, the whole program requires a commitment of less than twenty minutes a year." (Green, p.104). These books may overstate the case a bit, but they emphasize an important point. Passive investing is just that, passive. It should not involve a lot of intensive oversight, micromanagement or frequent portfolio changes. After all, as the chapter title says, we want it to be simple, disciplined, boring and profitable!

For those of you with a real interest in investing, I suggest you devote 80% of your investing time to the 20% of your money that is in your actively managed portfolio and about 20% of your time to the 80% of your money in the passively managed portfolio. I don't suggest you devote only a few minutes or few hours a year to your passive portfolio, but it should not take more than 20% of your investment time. Most of your time should be devoted to your actively managed portfolio, which we will examine in the next chapter.

Chapter 8
Beating the Market: It's Fun to Try

As indicated in the last chapter, I believe most of us should have a great deal of our investment money in a simple, disciplined foundation portfolio. A major reason for that is that most of us will feel more secure with our active investing and its usually higher level of risk if we know it is done on top of a good well-built foundation portfolio. While I think a foundation portfolio is essential for a complete investment strategy, I also enjoy active investing, stock picking and aggressive portfolio management as much as anyone else. I like to "beat the market," but that isn't my primary goal. As I get older, I am willing to take less risk with the market as a whole, and that is likely to affect my return relative to the market. I am also looking for more income than the total market will ordinarily provide, so my actively managed portfolio is likely to look different from that of the investor interested mainly in rapid growth. Specifically, my portfolio is oriented more toward stocks that will provide a good *and* rising, dividend return.

If you have a good foundation portfolio you should be willing o accept more risk with your actively managed investments. Before you start your active investing, you should have your basic financial planning goals in place. This would include having whatever money you are going to need for the next two or three years in very liquid assets such as short term bonds or bond funds, money market funds, savings accounts, certificates of deposit, Treasury bills, etc. These resources should also include sufficient resources to carry you through an emergency of up to six months, such as job loss, sudden illness, disabling accident, etc. If you have taken these steps and also have a foundation portfolio, you are ready to oversee an actively managed portfolio.

Picking Stocks

Picking stocks or other securities for your actively managed portfolio is a process in which you should be engaged all the time. As you read newspapers and periodicals, watch stock market channels on television or check out your favorite financial websites, look for stories or comments about companies that might represent potential investments. A company may be expanding its business in Asia or bringing out a new software package. Peter Lynch, the legendary manager of Fidelity Magellan in the 1980s and 1990s, used to say, "Invest in what you know."

You may be in a position to know a lot about a particular industry. If you live in the Detroit area, you may be very informed about the auto industry. If Las Vegas is your home, you may know a lot about the gaming, travel and entertainment industries. As you become familiar with sources of financial information, you will begin to see the same names mentioned again and again: IBM in the 1980s, Microsoft in the 1990s, Apple and

Google more recently. There is no guarantee that being mentioned in the press makes a stock a good investment, but it is a place to begin your research.

Publications like *Forbe's, Kiplinger's* and *Money* regularly identify stocks, bonds, mutual funds and other investments worth considering. *Money* has what it calls its "Money 70," a list of various categories of mutual funds that it recommends. The financial press, including *The Wall Street Journal, Barron's and Financial Times,* is an excellent source of information on potential investments.

I find *Morningstar, Standard and Poor's Outlook* and *Value Line* very helpful in choosing stocks and mutual funds because all three rank securities with a rating of one to five. Chapter 7 discusses the *Morningstar* ranking system. For *Morningstar* and *Outlook* a five-star designation is its best rating; a one-star is the lowest. *Value Line* reverses the system, and a rating of one is the highest evaluation. *Value Line* also breaks down its evaluation so that you can see its opinion of a stock's timeliness, safety and technical analysis position. *Value Line* and *Outlook* are not cheap but many public libraries have subscriptions that enable you to access the information. An advantage of *Morningstar* is that you can get most of the information without having to subscribe to the service. Their website provides detailed financial information, including the star rating, at no cost. You have to subscribe if you want to read their narrative analysis of a stock or fund. I personally think it is worth it to subscribe to their full service (it is the source I rely on more than any other), but it is certainly not necessary. All of the services also provide model portfolios and lists of favorite investments for your consideration.

When looking for a stock to fill a special need in my portfolio, I like to look at the portfolios of major mutual funds that invest in the kinds of stocks I am looking for. If I am looking for a growth stock, I look at the holdings of major growth funds. The same for value funds. For example, in the third quarter of 2011, the largest stock holdings of the Fidelity Growth Fund (FDGRX) and the Fidelity Value Fund (FDVLX) were as follows:

Fidelity Growth	Fidelity Value
Apple	Sempra Energy
Exxon Mobil	U.S. Bancorp
Salesforce.com	Wells Fargo
Google	Edison International
Red Hat	Berkshire-Hathaway

You will note the growth list is heavy on technical stocks, while the value list has a strong representation of utilities and financials. If you were looking for small cap, international or emerging markets stocks you could find them the same way, by looking at the appropriate mutual funds. One problem with the approach is that mutual fund managers are only required to report their portfolio holdings quarterly, so there may be some lag time between the time when they buy a stock and when you see it in their portfolio. This should not be a major problem for the long term investor, especially if you are looking at a fund that has relatively low portfolio turnover. You can find a fund's portfolio by looking at the prospectus or by going to the fund company website. The lists above, for example, are from www. fidelity.com. The major financial websites will also have the information available.

Major financial websites will also enable you to screen for the stocks that best meet your specific objectives. You might decide that you want to look only for stocks with an annual average earnings growth rate of at least 7%, a p/e ratio of less than

9, a dividend of at least 2% and an annual sales growth r.   .
at least 8% for 10 years. A screen like this would give you a list
of stocks to consider for investing. You might run such a screen
and then compare it with your list of stocks from the major mutual fund holdings. Once you get a short list of stocks like this
you can do your own homework and review them carefully before deciding to invest.

Looking at the Fundamentals

I am not an accountant and certainly not an expert at analyzing a company's financial statement. I expect most individual
investors are in a similar position. That does not mean that as individual investors we cannot do a reasonable job of understanding the fundaments of a company's financial position. My intention here is not to give you a comprehensive lesson on "how to
pick stocks." I am the wrong person for that. You should listen
to the advice and recommendations of people far more accomplished than me in choosing stocks for our portfolio. However, I
will address some of the factors that have been helpful to me in
selecting stocks over the years.

If I am interested in possibly buying a stock, I look first at
earnings. I look for a period of at least five years of increasing
earnings, but ten is better yet. Sometimes you have to allow for
special circumstances. In 2008 and 2009 many companies had
a dip in earnings because of the economic downturn, falling real
estate prices and other similar problems. If those years were
the only blemish on a decade of annually increasing earnings, I
would still consider the stock as a candidate for purchase.

Earnings alone tell you only part of the story. You need to
look also at how they relate to the stock's price, the price/earn-
ings ratio. This is a simple calculation achieved by dividing
the company's earnings into the stock price. A company with a

price of $10 and earnings of $1 has a p/e of 10 (otherwise stated as 10/1). A p/e can be helpful if it is compared to three benchmarks: (1) the general market; (2) the industry's p/e; and (3) the average historical p/e for the stock. Let us assume the XYZ Electric Company has the following characteristics:

XYZ Electric Company
Stock p/e	11/1
S&P500 p/e	16/1
Utility Industry p/e	12/1
XYZ Average Historical p/e	10/1

This tells us that XYZ's current p/e ratio is 11/1. This compares to a p/e for the general market as measured by the S&P500 of 16/1. Since utility companies usually are highly regulated and do not experience a high rate of price volatility or annual earnings increases, you would expect it to have a lower p/e than the general market. It is more useful to compare it to other companies in its own industry, i.e. utilities. In this case, the industry has a p/e of 12/1, so the XYZ p/e of 11/1 is not much different than the industry average. XYZ is also pretty much in line with its own historical average of 10/1. These numbers tell me that, taken as a whole, this utility is worth considering. It is no great bargain, but it is not overpriced and it might be something I would want to add to my stock holdings. I would also want to look at other items such as its dividend return and its record of increasing dividends over time.

One criticism of using earnings and p/e ratios in evaluating stocks is the charge that earnings can be manipulated to make the company look good. A maintenance or remodeling project can be delayed, or a company can let inventory get low without replacing it, and the actions will reduce current expenses, thereby increasing earnings in the current period. A company's chief financial officer may adjust its amortization or depreciation numbers. A bank may move more money to its reserve for loan losses, reducing its profits and its tax liability for a given period. These kinds of actions can be problems, but I don't think they render earnings numbers for stocks useless. They do emphasize the need to look at a company's long term, perhaps ten year, earnings trends. Also be aware if the numbers are historical or projected numbers. Historical earnings should have some factual basis, while projected earnings are someone's best guess, often wrong and usually too optimistic.

Another number I like to look at is the company's price/sales ratio. This number is calculated by dividing a company's total annual sales into total market value (share price multiplied by the number of shares outstanding). James O'Shaunessy, in his book, *What Works on Wall Street* (1998), found that this ratio is the best single predictor of future price movements. It is also much more difficult to manipulate than earnings. A company's annual sales number is a pretty specific amount, and is not subject to as much adjustment as noted above with earnings. There are no precise rules as to what is a good p/s ratio to look for. The ratios will vary greatly from company to company and industry to industry. In the third quarter of 2011, I looked at the largest company in each sector index fund representing the sectors of the S&P500. The results were as follows:

Price/Sales Ratios of S&P500 Sectors and Largest Company in Each Sector

Sector P/S		**Company P/S**	
Consumer discretionary	2.1	McDonald's	3.7
Consumer staples	1.8	Proctor & Gamble	2.3
Financials	1.3	JPMorgan	1.4
Utilities	1.5	Southern Co.	2.0
Energy	0.7	Exxon	0.8

Health care	2.8	Johnson&Johnson	2.8
Materials	1.0	E.I. DuPont	1.2
Technology	1.6	Apple	3.6
Industrials	0.9	Caterpillar	1.1
S&P500	1.3		

We can see that the p/s ratios ranged from 2.8 for the health care sector to 0.7 for the energy sector, while the general number for the S&P500 was 1.3. The most expensive stock relative to its sector was Apple, with a p/s ratio of 3.6 while the average for the tech sector was 1.6. None on the current list were below their sector average. As with the p/e ratio, the best use of the p/s ratio is to compare it with the general market (S&P500 or some other broad benchmark), with its sector and with its own historic trends.

I look first at price/earnings ratios and then at price/sales ratios when I am analyzing a stock. I sometimes look at the price/book ratio, but I use it less often than the others. *Investopedia* says that a company's book value is determined by calculating the company's total assets minus intangible assets (patents, goodwill, etc.) and liabilities. *Investopedia* also says another way of looking at price/book ratio is to consider it the total value of a company's assets that shareholders would theoretically receive if the company were to be liquidated. The price/book ratio is the company's price per share divided by the company's book value per share. Below are the price/book ratios of three companies, a consumer company (McDonald's), an industrial company (Caterpillar) and a technology company (IBM).

	2001	2006	2011
McDonalds	3.6	3.6	6.4
Caterpillar	6.5	6.1	4.5
IBM	9.1	5.3	9.3

The numbers by themselves tell you little. They need to be viewed in the context of what other companies in the same industry look like. A number of years ago I was involved in selling a bank of which I was a shareholder and member of the board of directors. I had helped found the bank a number of years earlier. We sold the bank for about three times book value. I was reluctant to sell because I was not sure we were receiving enough for the bank. Fortunately, my wiser colleagues brought me around to their point of view because many banks were then selling for 2.0 to 2.5 times book, and we were being offered a premium for our bank. A few years later, at the time of the financial crisis of 2008-10, many banks were lucky if they could demand a selling price of book value.

O'Shaunessy says that price/book ratios are useful at the extremes. Buying stocks when price/book values are very low compared with other stocks in the industry and with the stock's own history is often profitable. Extremely high price/book ratios, on the other hand, should be a warning sign. It is hard to fine tune book/values and make them a precise indicator for when to buy and sell.

Technical Analysis

Most investment analysts rely mainly on fundamental analysis, but technical analysts have a respectable following as well. Advocates of technical analysis argue that through the use of charts and the study of past stock prices over time, one can discern likely future price movements. This strategy has its critics, none more pointed than Burt Malkiel. In his *Random Walk,* he says:

> The results (of various studies he cites) reveal conclusively that past movements in stock prices cannot be used to foretell future movements. The

stock market has no memory. The central proposition of charting is absolutely false, and investors who follow its precepts will accomplish absolutely nothing but increasing substantially the brokerage they pay.

I will admit I don't know much about technical analysis. I would not want you deciding what you think about the subject based on my comments. I am not as critical as Malkiel, but I have found technical analysis strategies to be of only limited help in my investing, even though I do make some use of it. After I have decided I am interested in buying a stock, I look to technical analysis to help me know when to buy it. The tool I use most often is the 200 day moving average. If I want to buy a stock, but I find it is trading considerably above its moving average, I am likely to hold off buying for a while. At the very least I will want to do more research. I may then decide that the stock has moved above its moving average and is likely to keep right on going up, but the chart has caused me to take that second look.

I have never found so-called support levels or resistance levels to do me much good. This strategy seems to say something like the following:

> If the stock falls to its support level and goes through the level, it is likely to keep on falling.
> If it does not go through the support level, it is likely to stay above it.

I do n0t want to be unfair to my technician friends, of whom I have several, but I don't find that kind of information to be very helpful. You should do your research and make up your own mind about technical analysis. There are two technical analysts for whom I have much respect: John J. Murphy and John Bollinger, the creator of the Bollinger Bands. If you want to know more about the subject, I suggest you read some of their books or articles. I like Bollinger Bands because they help understand moving averages. They give an indication of how volatile a stock is as it fluctuates above and below its moving average.

Mutual Funds and Exchange Traded Funds

A well diversified actively managed portfolio can include mutual funds and exchange traded funds as well as stocks, bonds, cash equivalent investments, etc. They should be analyzed and chosen in the same way as other portfolio holdings. In addition, you will need to consider the usual criteria for picking funds— expense ratios, manager competence, etc. If you own a balanced fund, you will need to keep that in mind when analyzing your asset allocation for your next rebalancing. For example, a typical balanced fund might invest 60% in stocks and 40% in bonds. If you own such a fund you will need to allocate the appropriate portions to the different asset categories.

Some ETFs are so specialized that they are a good investment when you want to fill in a specific niche in your portfolio. If you need to own a Scandinavian technology fund or a small cap emerging markets fund, there is probably an ETF to meet your need. There is a joke that says there will soon be an ETF that owns companies specializing in diseases of the left lung and another that focuses on diseases of the right lung. Most of us don't have asset allocation plans with such specific categories, but the ETFs are there if you need them. I find that mutual funds and ETFs and useful to me in building my portfolio, but I know that some prefer to invest only in stocks and bonds. That is essentially a personal decision.

Control What You *Can* Control

There are many factors that can have an important impact on your portfolio over which you have no control—Federal Reserve policy, inflation rates, tax policy, commodity prices, etc. On the other hand, there are many factors impacting on your portfolio over which you can exercise control. If you give careful attention to these items, I believe you can add as much as 1% to your annual return. Some of them are listed below.

No-load funds -- When buying mutual funds, it is almost always to your benefit to buy no-load funds. A load (sales charge) on a fund adds nothing to performance. It goes to cover advertising and sales costs. If someone tries to tell you that load funds outperform no-load funds, you need to ask yourself, "What else is he lying to me about?" There may be a very few special cases where there is a reason to buy a load fund, but they are few and far between.

Brokerage fees -- In buying and selling securities you need to be sensitive to brokerage costs. It is likely that many of your transactions can be accomplished through discount or internet brokers, and will minimize your costs in the process. You may need a full service broker for certain types of transactions. I use one to help me select municipal bonds for the bond portion of my portfolio because that is not an area where I feel competent making decisions on my own. I am glad to compensate him for that service. Many times all I need to do is implement a decision I have made to buy or sell a stock, and in those cases, I can achieve everything I want to do through the use of an internet broker.

Employer matching contributions -- Although not as common as it once was, many employers still match part of an employee's contributions to a retirement account, 401k, 403b, etc.

The most common pattern seems to be for employers to match an employee's contributions up to a maximum of 3%. In such a plan, if an employee puts 6% in his retirement account, then along with the employer contribution, a total of 9% will go into the account.

I sometimes hear people say they do not like their employer's retirement plan for some reason, often because they are unhappy with the selection of funds offered by the plan. Rather they prefer to invest in an individual retirement account on their own. This is almost always a bad decision. If an employer is willing to match contributions, so that $1 being invested by the employee results in $2 being invested in the account, it is almost impossible for the individual to do as well investing on their own without the match. At the very least the individual should invest in the plan up to the limit of the match. Then if they want to invest in their own IRA after that, it would be wise to do so. Do not leave dollars on the table that your employer is willing to invest on your behalf.

Low turnover -- There is much research that shows that low portfolio turnover is closely related to superior portfolio return. This is just another way of saying that low portfolio expenses are a big help in improving investment results. No loads, low annual expenses and low turnover are all part of the same strategy. Turnover increases portfolio costs. If you are buying and selling frequently for your portfolio, you are generating portfolio costs (mainly brokerage charges) and may also be generating tax liabilities. It is wise to trade as little as possible. If you trade frequently, be sure you pay the lowest possible brokerage fees, and take advantage of special discounts many brokers offer to frequent traders.

If you are trading mutual funds, be aware of the turnover rate of the funds. A fund with a turnover rate of 100% means that, on average, every stock owned by the fund trades once a year. If the turnover rate is 50% the fund has had an average of one trade for every two funds. Index and tax-managed funds usually have the lowest turnover rates. As an example, Vanguard Total Stock Market Index Fund and Vanguard Total International Stock Index Fund were reporting turnover rates of 3.0% late in 2011. The conservative actively managed T. Rowe Price Equity Income Fund had an 8.5% turnover rate. You can expect more aggressive funds to have somewhat higher rates. The Fidelity Growth Appreciation Fund and Janus Enterprise Fund both reported 23%. All of these numbers are reasonable for the kinds of funds they are. You can find turnover rates in reports from the fund or on most major financial websites.

Tax deferrals and tax exemption -- You can have considerable control over your tax liabilities. The best way to defer your tax obligations is to take advantage of plans such as 401k and 403b plans offered by your employer or individual retirement accounts that you can manage on your own. Money you set aside for education can also be tax-deferred. Education 529 plans are your best bet because they allow large amounts, as much as $300,000 in some cases, to be invested and used for educational purposes, with the taxes deferred until the money is actually withdrawn and spent. Coverdell education savings accounts are also available, but the amounts you can invest annually are much smaller. Beginning in 2013 your annual maximum investment will be just $500. If you own U.S. Savings Bonds, and you spend the interest on educational expenses, those expense payments are tax deductible.

Even more desirable than tax deferral programs are those that are tax exempt, where you never pay taxes. Municipal bonds are a good example. These are bonds issued by cities, counties, states, school districts, public universities, etc. These bonds pay lower interest rates than high grade corporate bonds, so whether it makes sense for you to own them depends on what income bracket you are in. You should get advice from your tax advisor as to whether it is advantageous for you to own municipal bonds.

A very attractive plan for long term investors is the Roth individual retirement account. With this plan you contribute after-tax dollars to your Roth IRA, and then you *never* pay taxes on the money you withdraw. Annual contribution limits change from time to time, but in 2012 you and your spouse can contribute $5000 or $6000 if you are over age 50. You must also have earned income equal to or greater than the amount you contribute to the Roth. There are income limits that determine whether you can contribute to these accounts. Your adjusted gross income should be less than $105,000 for a single person or $167,000 for married couples. Your eligibility phases out as your income rises above these levels. The Roth is a great program for those who qualify for them. Don't pass up the opportunity to have one if you are eligible.

Managing Your Portfolio

Managing your portfolio is an ongoing process. An actively managed portfolio does not manage itself, and neglecting it can be an expensive mistake. Warren Buffet is often quoted as saying he has two rules for investing:

> Rule #1: Don't lose what you already have
> Rule #2: Don't forget Rule #1

It is imperative that you have a few basic strategies in mind for protecting your portfolio values. Asset allocation is the first, and most important, strategy (You are probably getting tired of hearing this). This strategy assures you that, when the stock market falls sharply, the portion of your portfolio not in the stock market will be protected from market volatility.

I also like to decide ahead of time how much loss I am willing to take on my larger stock and fund holdings. There is no specific strategy here, but I usually set a point 15% to 20% below the current price. If I own Widget Manufacturing, and I am convinced it is a solid long-term holding, I may set a sell price about 20% below the current price. If the price falls 5%, 10%, or 15%, and I am still convinced it is a good holding, I do nothing. If it falls 20%, I accept the fact that the market knows something I do not know. I will then sell a portion I have determined, perhaps half, two-thirds or all of the holding. I am aware of the shortcoming of this strategy. Immediately after I sell, the price of Widget may reverse and start climbing sharply again. If it does, I just accept the fact, and am satisfied that I had limited my loss to no more than 20%. The strategy protects me from much larger losses.

If I make such a sale, I leave the money in cash until I am ready to reenter the market. That may not be until rebalancing time. There is nothing magic about a 15% or 20% sell point. William O'Neill, publisher of *Investor's Business Daily,* often uses an 8% figure. For my portfolio, that would create more turnover than I am comfortable with, but the important point is that there is no absolute right or wrong number. Use a number you are comfortable with.

Some people set sell points based on moving averages. If you use technical analysis, this might appeal to you. You might, for example, decide that you will sell if the stock falls more than X% below its moving average, or if it falls below its Bollinger Band limits. As with so much of investing, the important point here is discipline. Set your sell points before the market plunge begins, and then discipline yourself to implement them when the time comes.

Sometimes I sell a stock because it goes up. I am uneasy when any one stock or fund constitutes more than 10% of my portfolio. Therefore, if it reaches that point, I begin to sell it off to keep it within the 10% guideline. You may be reluctant to sell a stock if you see it rising rapidly in price. In that case, you might let the price run up, but set a very tight sell point, perhaps just a 5% drop, for getting out.

I also like to maintain a "potential buy list" in case stocks drop sharply. On those occasions when the bottom drops out of the market as it does sometimes (October, 1987 or September-December, 2008), all stocks, good and bad, are likely to fall. I like to have a list ready to add to my holdings when stocks go "on sale."

Each year at rebalancing time, I also try to upgrade my portfolio. By that I mean eliminate those investments that no longer seem to fit. Stocks sometimes have stock dividends, or spinoffs of some company they own. This may leave me with a small odd number of shares of a company I don't really want. I sometimes refer this as the "dribs and drabs" in my portfolio. At that point I have to decide if I want to own these shares. If I like the new company that has been spun off, I may buy more shares so that I have a significant number. That happened a few years ago when Pepsico spun off Yum Corp., its subsidiary that owned Taco Bell, KFC and Pizza Hut. I received a few shares of Yum from the spinoff and then bought more. It turned out to be a good decision as Yum has done well, especially in China and other emerging market locations.

Near the end of the year, when I am rebalancing, I sometimes find that I own something that has gone nowhere. It is something I thought would be a good investment, and I turned out to be wrong. That is a good time to clean up and upgrade the portfolio by selling such holdings. I wish I could say I never have such stocks or funds among my investments, but that would not be the case.

Active management of a portfolio is serious business. It takes time and effort. CNBC's Jim Cramer says that when it comes to monitoring and managing portfolios, investors should devote one hour a week for each stock or fund they own. That seems a bit high to me, but I agree with him that overseeing investments takes time. You may pay a high price in financial losses if you ignore or pay little attention to your portfolio. If you don't have the time and the interest, or don't want to devote it to your portfolio, then you should rely more on your broker or financial advisor. This is also a good reason for having more of your investment assets in your passively managed foundation portfolio.

Chapter 9
Being Your Own Financial Planner
Or Knowing How to Choose One

Investing should always be done within a larger context that includes one's current financial situation, future goals, retirement plans, etc. My intention in this book is to emphasize investing more than the general subject of financial planning, but I want to include a general discussion of financial planning for two reasons. First, investors need to consider their general financial planning goals in developing their investment strategies. Second, investors need to decide how much of their financial planning they want to do for themselves and how much they want to rely on others. Through the years I have done much of my investing and financial planning myself, but I also use a broker, accountant and an attorney when appropriate.

Taking a Financial Inventory

Financial planning should begin with understanding where you are now. I recommend you do a financial inventory similar to that shown in Figure 9.1. I begin by making a list of everything I own. I then divide the list into two parts, use assets and investment assets. Use assets are the things we use today—house, cars, personal items, etc. Investment assets are those things we own for use in the future—an investment portfolio, education accounts, retirement accounts, life insurance, etc. The use asset and investment asset categories of the financial inventory should show the value of everything my wife and I own. Then, we need to calculate all of our debts and subtract them from our assets to determine our net worth.

Figure 9.1

Net Worth Statement for John and Mary Saver
Use Assets

Auto I	$ 18,000
Auto II	6,000
House	240,000
Furniture	20,000
Personal Items	14,000
Boat	$ 8,000

Total Use Assets $306,000

Investment Assets

Equities

ABC Growth Fund $	18,100
DEF Value Fund	13,200
100 sh GHI Co.	14,300

(Continued on next page)

120

200 sh XYZ Co.		16,300	
	$	61,900	(55.2%)

Bonds and Fixed Income
PDQ Bond Fund	$	15,300	(13.6%)

Cash and Cash Equivalents
Checking Account	$	12,000	
Cert. of Deposit		8,000	
Life Ins. Cash Value		1,000	
	$	21,000	(18.7%)

Investment Assets
Real Estate
Lmtd Partnership	$	10,000	(8.9%)

Precious Metals
Gold Bullion	$	4,000	(3.6%)
Total Invest. Assets	$	112,200	(100.0%)

Total Assets	$	430,200

Debts
Mortgage	$	85,000
Credit Cards		1,400
Auto I Loan		3,000
Total Debts	$	89,400

Net Worth
(Total assets less debt)$ 340,800

In the data in Figure 9.1, John and Mary have assets worth $430,200 and debts of $89,400, so their net worth is $340,800.

The chart is just for your use. Your accountant, attorney or others are not using it, so don't worry about "getting it right" to satisfy them. If you are not sure where to put at item, put it where it makes the most sense to you. If you want to get more sophisticated, you can include, under investment assets, such items as the capitalized value of your Social Security income, annuity payouts or a guaranteed pension program. Doing so would involve estimating the values of these assets based on current interest rates. I personally do not include them because I do not find it helpful in doing my own financial planning. However, an accountant can make a good case for inclusion.

I like to take a financial inventory once a year, usually in January, using my year-end financial statements, but it can be done any time. When I go to a shopping center and look at a map of the center, the first thing I want to find is the designation, "You are here." That is the first step in deciding where I want to go. When you are doing financial planning, your net worth statement is the map that tells you, "You are here."

Tracking Where It Comes From and Where It Goes

I am not a strong advocate of dollar-by-dollar, day-by-day budgeting, mainly because most people will not do it even though they begin with the best of intentions. I do believe it is good to have a general knowledge of your income and spending patterns over time. Begin with a listing of your income, which may or may not include some of the following:

Salary	Dividend income
Spouse salary	Rental income
Commissions	Social Security
Second job income	Retirement income
Interest income	

If you have income that cannot be depended on to be there every month, perhaps commissions or a second job, you are better off not including them in your estimated income if you can do so.

There is no way to suggest to you the proper amount of income you should spend on various expense categories. I looked at several books and websites that contain information about family budgets, and based on the information gathered, I created Figure 9.2. which I call a "typical" budget, not the "right" budget. That first response of many looking at Figure 9.2 will be to say, "Well, that doesn't apply to me." They will almost certainly be correct. About the only generalization one can make about budgets is that every situation will be unique. If you have two children in college, your budget is likely to look at lot different than if you have two children in elementary school. If you live in San Francisco or New York City, your housing expenses may well be over 50% of your income. If you, or someone for whom you are financially responsible, has special medical needs, your health care expenses will be higher than for others. If you want to do some research on your own, you can google such subjects as family finance, family budgets, etc. Morningstar has a good budget worksheet on its website. Go to "real life finance," then to "family finance" and then on to "budget worksheet."

There is an old proverb that is stated in different ways, but it goes like this:

Income	:	$100
Expenses:		$ 99
Result:		Satisfaction

Income	:	$100
Expenses:		$101
Result:		Frustration

Figure 9.2

"Typical" Family Budget

Income (after taxes)
Salary	$ 40,000
Spouse salary	28,000
Second job	8,000
Interest	4,000
Total Income	**$ 80,000**

Expenses
Food (11%)	$ 8,800
Housing (35%)	28,000
Transportation (15%)	12,000
Health care (10%)	8,000
Education entertainment (5%)	4,000
Personal, clothing (4%)	3,200
Contributions (8%)	6,400
Investments, retirement (12%)	9,600
Total Expenses	**$ 80,000**

Doing some of your own financial planning begins with an understanding of your current financial situation and managing your finances. Keeping your expenses less than your income is key.

Goals and Strategies

After you decide where you are financially, you need to decide where you want to go. Typical financial goals would include:

> Providing for retirement
> Purchasing a home
> Providing for children's educational needs
> Starting a business
> Buying a second, or vacation, home

These are in no particular order other than that I have put providing for retirement first. This may seem strange to a 25 or 35 year old, but as life expectancy is extended, and retirement plans depend more on the individual and less on employers or government, a secure retirement depends on lifelong planning. If you have to choose, I would put it above providing for a child's education. In the long run, the best gift you can give your children is the assurance they will not have to support you in your later years.

Goals should have timetables. You may plan to buy a house in five years, send children to college in twelve years and retire in twenty-five years. This means each will occupy a different place in your portfolio. Your long-term holdings can be invested more heavily in higher risk investments such as stocks. This is another area where we see the special issues associated with providing for retirement. Within limits, we can determine the age at which we retire. We have no way of knowing how long the retirement period itself will last. I usually tell people with whom I am working on financial planning that, to be safe, they should assume a life span of 95. If they insist that males in their family have a history of death in the 50s from heart attack (or some other story), I may relent a bit. I would still urge using the 95 year assumption in most cases, as one of basic purposes of retirement planning is to assure that we do not outlive our financial resources. As I have said earlier, money you will need in the next two or three years should not be in the stock market, but rather in short-term bond funds, money market funds, Treasuries, certificates of deposit, etc. Other investments should reflect the timetable of the goals to be achieved.

Monitoring, Reviewing and Revising

Our financial situation is never static. It changes constantly and needs to be monitored on a continuing basis. If you have mainly a passive (or index) portfolio, it will not, and should not, take a lot of your time for monitoring. Your active portfolio will take somewhat more time, but even there, micromanaging on a day-to-day basis is likely to do more harm than good.

A comprehensive financial review should be done regularly, preferably annually. This should include not just a portfolio rebalancing and the other things I have mentioned but also a review of goals. Changes in life can cause goals to change: marriage, divorce, birth of a child, change of employment, serious illness, retirement. Time itself causes goals to change as we are presented with life changes we cannot foresee.

Information Resources for the Individual Investor

Individuals doing their own financial planning or investment management have more resources available to them than at any time in history. No one has time to use all of them. It is a matter of choosing what is most effective for you.

Books -- I have discussed a number of books in these pages, and there are dozens of outstanding investment books, with new ones coming out all the time. There are a very few that I would describe as classics in that they describe the fundamental, universal principles that apply to investment generally rather than to specific securities, traits or strategies. Any list is somewhat arbitrary, but here is where I would start.

My Five Favorites

Benjamin Graham, *The Intelligent Investor*
Burton Malkiel, *Random Walk Down Wall Street*
John Bogle, *Common Sense on Mutual Funds*
Jeremy Siegel, *Stocks for the Long Run*
William Bernstein, *The Intelligent Asset Allocator*

Like the Rose Bowl in college football, Graham's book, *The Intelligent Investor,* is the "granddaddy of them all" when it comes to investment books. Thousands of college students have been introduced to investments through Benjamin Graham and David Dodd's textbook, *Security Analysis,* first published in 1934. This more general version of that book, by Graham, was published in 1949.

I have already referred to Malkiel's book, *Random Walk,* many times because I think it presents the most carefully researched and clearly stated explanation of how markets work. I am not a purist when it comes to believing in the total randomness of markets, but I think it explains much of how markets operate. For me, this is the single most important guide for my own long-term investing.

I have listed Bogle's book, *Common Sense on Mutual Funds,* because it is a comprehensive presentation of his views. If you would prefer a more compact book, his *Little Book of Common Sense Investing* is a good choice. All of Bogle's books are a good complement to Malkiel's book. They help you know how to use the information you find in *Random Walk.*

Jeremy Siegel, in *Stocks for the Long Run,* makes the case for stocks being the best investment for the long-term investor. He presents an abundance of evidence, going back over 200 years, and shows relationships between large stocks, small stocks, bonds, inflation, etc.

I have emphasized asset allocation time and again, and no one knows that subject better than William Bernstein. His *The Intelligent Asset Allocator* is the authoritative work on the subject.

I have selected these books, but there are so many worth reading. I would include all the following as really worthwhile for the serious individual investor.

Dick Davis, *The Dick Davis Dividend*
Charles Ellis, *Investment Policy: How to Win the Loser's Game*
Richard Ferri, *The Power of Passive Investing*
Justin Fox, *The Myth of the Rational Market*
Alexander Greene, *The Gone Fishin' Portfolio*
Richard Lehman, *Far From Random*
James O'Shaughnessy, *What Works on Wall Street*
Allan Roth, *How a Second Grader Beats Wall Street*
Daniel Solin, *The Smartest Investment Book You Will Ever Read*

Periodicals -- If I were going to read just one financial magazine, it would be either *Kiplinger's Personal Finance* or *Money Magazine.* Both have good solid information, and both are written for the general reader. They have articles such as "What to Do With $1,000 Now," "The Best Stocks to Buy for Your Children," or "The Ten Best Mutual Funds to Buy Now." *Forbes* includes much of the same type of material, but it is perhaps a bit more sophisticated than the other two. If you want to do most of your own investment research, this is a good choice for you. All three of them regularly publish lists of recommended stocks and mutual funds for purchase, such as the "Money 70" or the "Kiplinger's 25" lists, but as most of the research in this book points out, it is difficult for them to consistently outperform the market over the long run.

For the individual who wants to do more in-depth stock market research, I strongly recommend the *AAII Journal*, a monthly publication of the American Association of Individual Investors. All of the printed material of the organization, as well as the vast array of information on the website, is available for the modest annual membership costs of AAII. I believe the organization is a must for serious individual investors.

The Economist is a high quality, general purpose publication that covers economic, business and financial news worldwide. It is based in London and has staff in this country, but it reports worldwide, not just from Europe and the United States. It provides a broad perspective on the subjects it addresses, but often it also has special inserts that address one subject intensely. Subjects might be a country or region or perhaps a specific topic such as European debt or development issues in Africa. Canadian investors cannot do better than reading the monthly, *Canadian Money Saver.* This publication, founded by Dale and Betty Ennis over three decades ago, is committed to helping the individual investor. *Consumer Reports* is a somewhat different publication, emphasizing the evaluation of products for consideration by consumers. It does, however, offer information on financial products that will be of interest to investors. It might include articles on bank fees, mutual fund expenses or abuses in the financial industry.

If you are looking for a pure data source, with an abundance of information on long-term market patterns, history of the major indexes, etc. you will want the *Stock Trader's Almanac*. If you want to find detailed information on such trends as the presidential election cycle or the "sell in May and go away" phenomenon, this is the place to look. I would call this a periodical because it is published regularly on an annual basis. I find it to be essential in my work, since I rely on it to get information for the publication of our monthly newsletter and also use it in doing research for my own portfolio.

Newspapers -- Traditional newspapers still provide an essential core of information for investors, with the *Wall Street Journal* as the "bible" of the industry. If you don't read the *Journal* for the information in it, you read it to see what the nation's CEOs and financial gurus are reading when they first get up in the morning. In addition to news, it has a strong editorial and opinion section that speaks regularly to public policy issues from a business point of view. *Barron's*, a weekly publication is published by the same company and covers much of the same information. One difference is that many of the *Barron's* articles are to provide a specific opinion on the companies being discussed. From time to time, it will then publish follow-up articles indicating how accurate it was in its original analysis of the companies, as to whether they have gone up or down in price.

Investor's Business Daily is perhaps the major competitor to the *Journal*. It includes considerably more statistical information and data that will be of use to those doing fundamental and technical market analysts. It has somewhat fewer articles on general business and economic issues.

The *Financial Times* is to the newspaper world what the *Economist* is for periodicals. Based in London, and easily recognized by its unique buff color, it covers the world with an emphasis on Europe. *Financial Times* has Washington based staff and also provides comprehensive coverage of U.S. issues. In quality it is at least the equal of all the other newspapers mentioned above.

Television -- As with so much of the media today, television plays an ever more important role. CNBC is the prominent player. It has knowledgeable staff and professional programming. It has reputable, long-time staff like Bill Griffith, Sue Herrera and Maria Bartiromo, who have been with them for years. They are also known for colorful commentators like the opinionated Larry Kudlow and the excitable Jim Cramer. Bloomberg News is an equally credible network. When it comes to 24 hour international news, it may be even stronger than CNBC. Pimm Fox is one of their strongest hosts, Al Hunt does political news and Charlie Rose does general interest interviews. Fox Business Channel is an up-and-coming network, but it has a ways to go to compete with the two others. Neil Cavuto, formerly with CNBC, is their best known on-air personality. Public television has a first-rate evening thirty-minute program, Nightly Business Report. It presents a concise summary of the day's economic and market news five nights a week. If you are limited as to the amount of time you want to devote to business and markets,, this is the program for you.

It is essential to keep in mind that the guests on all these programs are there for one primary reason. They want to get exposure for themselves and their firms. Whether they are right in their comments (whatever "right" means) is less important than their images being on the screen. They are also almost always more oriented toward short-term trading than is appropriate for most individual investors. For example, when they make a statement such as, "Investors should be moving into smaller companies in emerging market countries," there is no way of knowing whether they mean for six months or two or three years. Listen to what they have to say, but remember they have no special ability to predict the future.

Websites-- The internet world moves so rapidly, a list of today's best websites will likely be somewhat out of date by the time you read this. Nevertheless, there are some that are of such quality they are likely to be the leaders for some time to come. I have already noted that I use www.morningstar.com more than any other website. It covers the entire investment world and provides a wealth of information. For a modest annual fee (less than $200 in 2012), you can subscribe to their premium service that provides a comprehensive list of screening and analytical tools for monitoring, analyzing and managing your portfolio. Their free basic service, however, offers plenty of data and tools to enable investors to do serious research on all aspects of their portfolios—stocks, bonds, funds, etfs, personal finance, etc.

The finance sections of www.yahoo.com and www.aol.com are both comprehensive and very good. The site www.money. cnn.com is sponsored by CNN, *Money* and *Fortune* magazines. It often supplements information found in the magazines. The site www.marketwatch.com is similar, with a strong combination of information and columnists who offer informed opinion on the markets and economy. As noted above, the American Association of Individual Investors has a strong website to supplement its monthly magazine. It is best to play around with the sites and see which best meets your needs.

There are more specialized sites you may want to check. You should check out www.bankrate.com as the best source of information on all matters concerning interest rates—corporate and government, municipals, money markets, mortgages, certificates of deposit, etc. Depending on what you are looking for, it enables you to compare rates to find the product that best meets your needs. If you do charting of your holdings, you will want to look at www.stockcharts.com and www.bigcharts.com. Both include a long list of tools that provide a basis for technical analysis. The bigcharts website also has a history option so that you can find the price of a stock on any given day going back many years. It includes such information as stock splits, which can be very helpful to you if you are trying to calculate your original cost for tax purposes.

Finally, the websites of the large mutual fund companies are a rich source of information. Sites like fidelity.com, vanguard.com and troweprice.com all offer data, tools and general information for planning and evaluation. They do not limit their information to just their own funds, but enable you to compare with other fund company products as well. They usually also have an on-line brokerage service available, with low fees and access to all types of securities.

My Favorite Information Sources

Over time most of us develop a set of sources we respect and to which we pay special attention. This is a personal choice, but I will mention some I enjoy reading or listening on a regular basis. If you are interested in how accurate newsletters are with their predictions, Mark Hulbert is the best in the business. Mark is the "dean" of newsletter performance, with his *Hulbert Financial Digest* and his regular articles in marketwatch.com. He compares newsletter performance on both an absolute and a risk-adjusted basis, and he provides the information for varying time periods, up to twenty years.

On the subject of mutual funds, no one knows the business better than Chuck Jaffe. He provides both news and commentary in his *Boston Globe* and syndicated columns as well as in his on-line columns at www.marketwatch.com. He also does a Boston based radio show. He is especially well known for his "stupid investment" series, in which he calls attention to the scandals and foibles of the industry, but he has both a broad background and a depth of understanding of mutual funds and the world of finance. Not surprisingly from what I have said earlier, I find anything written by Burt Malkiel or John Bogle to be worth reading. In recent years, Bogle has become more critical of the mutual fund industry and the financial world in general. His criticisms in *The Battle for the Soul of Capitalism* (2006) are on target and worth considering.

Christine Benz, who writes regularly for www.morningstar. com, is one of the best of the newer contributors to financial literature. She has put much of her work in her book, *30 Minute Money Solutions* (2011), and she is always adding new material through her on-line articles. I am impressed with her work. Finally, I especially like the five-day-a-week syndicated radio show hosted by Ray Lucia of San Diego. Ray is a certified financial planner and retirement specialist who hosts his daily show along with a "brain trust" that includes an attorney and another financial planner who join him in answering questions called in by his listeners. He also offers free seminars at various locations around the country. You can go to his website, www. raylucia.com, to find what radio station in your area carries his program. You probably have your own list of favorite sources. If not, then until you do, I invite you to check out some of mine.

Choosing a Financial Planner

Many investors like to do much of their own financial planning, but there will also be times when they want to get some professional help. Choosing the right person can be tricky because in most states the term "financial planner" is a generic term with little specific meaning. Attorneys, brokers, insurance agents, tax preparers or almost anyone else can hang out a sign and they are in the business. With that in mind, there are some things for you to consider in choosing the right person to help you.

First, you will want to know the formal education and credentials of your potential planners. The most common designation is Certified Financial Planner. This means the individual has completed a course of study and passed exams on a series of subjects including investing, insurance, taxation, estate and general financial planning. It also means that they keep up to date through regular continuing education programs that they are required to take. This is the designation I first studied for in the 1980s. Another designation you may find is Chartered Financial Analyst. This tells you the holders of this title have completed an extensive course of study of corporate finance and corporate stocks. If you are looking for someone to help you in picking individual stocks and understanding financial operations rather than more general financial planning assistance, this is likely the person for you.

Second, you should ask potential planners about their experience. Although a certified financial planner is broadly educated, most will have more experience in some areas than others. One may specialize in insurance, another in investing, still another in taxation. You can also ask them what kind of clients they are most experienced in working with. Some work only with high net worth individuals, perhaps those with assets of $5 million or more. Others will work mainly with middle income professionals who want assistance in managing their 401k, 403b or IRA accounts. Be sure any planner you choose is a good fit for your needs.

Third, you should understand a planner's employment status. Are they self-employed, do they work for a broker, mutual fund company or other financial institution? You will want to know if there are limits on the services they can provide you. For example, you do not want a planner who can only sell you their employer's financial products. If they can only offer you the firm's insurance plans, mutual funds or annuities, you should look elsewhere for assistance. Be sure they are free to offer you the full range of stocks, bonds, mutual funds, exchange-traded funds or other securities without regard to who created or distributes the products.

Fourth, you should understand how the planner is compensated. There are a variety of legal and ethical ways for planners to be paid, and you should ask the potential planner to describe the compensation plan with you. Some are fee-only financial planners. Others, who are paid by commissions, will charge lower or no fees, but they are paid based on the financial products you buy. Some planners are paid by a combination of the two, while others offer consultation based on an hourly fee basis. If all you need is a general overview of your portfolio, or perhaps answers to specific questions, this may be a good alternative. In my own rather limited financial planning practice, some of the most satisfying work I do is with modest income individuals, often teachers, who just need to be pointed in the right direction. They can get what they need just paying for a one or two hour consulting session, perhaps annually or semi-annually.

In discussing compensation, you have a right to ask planners to see their Securities and Exchange ADV Form, Part II. This form explains their compensation system, and it also should list any potential conflicts of interest the planner may have. Most professional planners will be expecting this question and will not be offended when asked.. They will likely have the form readily available for your review.

Finally, consistent with the ideas I have emphasized throughout these pages, I would question potential planners about their general investing philosophy. Do they believe in the use of index funds? Are they committed to using mutual and exchange-traded funds with the lowest possible annual expenses? Do they understand and support asset allocation and annual rebalancing? On the other hand, do they make any claims that raise a red flag in your mind? Do they claim to have special proprietary strategies that will help you "beat the market?" Remember, if what they promise you sounds too good to be true, it probably is!

There are websites that will help you find a good financial planner. Go to www.cfp.net to find a certified financial planner. If you are looking for a fee-only planner, check out www.napfa.org. You will find information on chartered financial analysts at www.cfainstitute.org. Good luck.

Chapter 10
Preparing for the Future:
Retirement and Beyond

Throughout this book I have written based on my sixty years of experience in the stock market. Valid or not, I have assumed that those years of experience might give me something to say about investing. This chapter is different. I am now retired; I entered retirement just as everyone else does, with no prior experience in the process. It is a trial and error activity, of which I will share some of my experiences and thoughts as I entered retirement. Keep in mind that I claim no expertise, and I find retirement to be a continual learning process.

When to Retire

The first question we face about retirement is when to do so. I retired in my mid-sixties. Some who are financially able retire much sooner. After a decade in which the Dow Jones Industrial Average, S&P500 and other major indexes have gone essentially nowhere, many people are finding they have little choice but to delay retirement to nearer seventy or beyond. The retirement decision involves considering both what we want to do and what we can afford to do. Of course, many financial decisions involve those same two considerations.

Retirement need not be an either/or decision. When I retired, I made an agreement with the university to phase into retirement with a 67% contract my first year, 33% contract my second year and then I completely retired at the end of the second year. Then, in retirement, I continued to teach one course a year for several years. Outside the university, I continued to have a small financial planning practice and to co-edit our newsletter, *No-Load Portfolios*. When invited, I also continued lecturing at various financial conferences and seminars around the country.

It appears that more people are making retirement a gradual process rather than moving abruptly from full-time employment to total retirement. As I visit with fellow retirees, I have come to appreciate the fact that retirement should not be defined as not working, but rather as "doing what you want to do." If a person wants to cut off all connections with their prior working years and spend their time fishing, golfing or playing tennis that is what they should do. If they want to do volunteer work, they should. If they want to work part-time because they want to work, they have to work or they want a more financially comfortable retirement, then that is what they should do.

Social Security

A major consideration for many people in deciding when to retire is how much Social Security income they will receive in retirement. The amount they receive will depend to a large extent on the age at which they choose to begin receiving Social Security benefits. Age 62 is the earliest possible age, but if a beneficiary chooses to delay receiving benefits until they are close to age 70, they can increase their income by a third or more. The longer one waits, the more monthly income they will receive.

Retirees planning to work part-time should remember that earned income can cause them to lose some of their Social Security payments. If an individual chooses to receive Social Security benefits prior to reaching their full retirement age (currently 66), they will forfeit $1 of benefits for every $2 they earn over $14,160 annually.

Social security benefits are available not just to direct recipients but also to widows, widowers, certain disabled individuals and minor children. It is particularly important to be aware of spousal benefits. In some cases the benefits of one can increase the benefits of the other. Social Security is a subject on which you will want to do your homework before making important decisions such as when to begin receiving benefits. The agency's website, www.ssa.gov, provides valuable information that will be helpful to you in making your decisions. The American Association of Retired Persons' website, www.aarp.com, is also a good source of information. It has both a Social Security calculator and a general retirement calculator available. Most mutual fund websites have a wealth of retirement information. I especially like www.troweprice.com.

Social Security: A Personal Note

I have read that more people in their thirties today believe we have been visited by aliens from other planets than believe Social Security will be there for them when they retire. If they really believe that, they are simply wrong. We are not going to wake up some morning and see a headline that says, "Social Security Goes Bankrupt." Rather, we will see over a period of years a series of adjustments that will reduce somewhat the value of benefits. As more of our population mature and retire, Social Security will face a series of financial challenges, but they are not insurmountable. It is likely that the age of eligibility for full benefits and the formula for calculating the cost-of-living increases will be adjusted. Those in their working years are likely to find that the amount of their income subject to Social Security tax will be raised, and wealthier individuals will find their benefits limited (but not eliminated) if they have other retirement income. None of these changes will be welcome, but they are the kind of reforms that will strengthen and protect Social Security. I am certain today's thirty-five year olds will see a Social Security check before they see a visitor from Mars!

On the other hand, today's workers in their thirties, forties or fifties need to remember the primary purpose of Social Security. From the beginning in the 1930s, it was intended to provide a base on which individuals could build a retirement plan and investment programs that will provide a comfortable lifestyle in retirement. Social Security was never intended to be the major source of retirement income, although for too many people it is. If I were giving the Social Security Administration advice, I would recommend that every document that leaves the agency, every brochure, letter, annual report to recipients, etc. contain a statement at the top of the page that says, in bold letters, something like the following:

> Social Security is not intended to provide most of your retirement income. You are strongly encouraged to take advantage of employer plans, individual retirement accounts and other programs designed to provide an adequate income during your retirement years.

I doubt that will occur, but it is worth thinking about.

Other Retirement Accounts

Hopefully you have created other retirement accounts in addition to your Social Security, perhaps traditional or Roth IRAs, 401k's, 403b's, etc. Earlier in the book we talked about investment strategies that can be used to build up the balance in your retirement accounts. As you approach retirement, the process gets reversed. In retirement you need to decide how best to withdraw money from your accounts so as to provide adequate retirement income while also minimizing the impact of taxes.

There are two questions retirees and soon-to-be retirees talk about when they get together. The first is how much can they afford to withdraw from their retirement accounts each year without eventually running out of money. The second is in what order should money be withdrawn from the various accounts. In the go-go stock market years of the 1990s, it was common for financial planners to suggest you could withdraw 7% or 8% annually. Today, after a decade of essentially flat stock market returns, individuals are much more conservative in their income projections. There is no one answer to the question because there is no one set of assumptions on which to base projections. The most widely used assumption today seems to be that one can safely withdraw 4% annually and, after the first year of retirement, make annual inflation adjustments of about 2.5%. For example, if you have $500,000 available for retirement, you would be able to withdraw $20,000 (4%) the first year, and then adjust 2.5% annually. That would provide $20,500 the second year, $21,012 the third year, etc. If you retire in your early sixties, you may want to withdraw less than 4% in your early retirement years, but if you are not retiring until your early or mid-seventies, it is probably safe for you to begin with withdrawals for more than 4%.

An important advantage for retirees is that they are not making a once-and-forever decision. If you withdraw 4% for a few years, and then feel that you are spending down your account balance too rapidly, you can reduce the amount of your annual withdrawals. As with Social Security, you can get plenty of help doing your retirement homework. Morningstar's website has a retirement worksheet you can use, and troweprice.com website has a superior retirement section, with tools and calculators to help you estimate retirement income using different assumptions you can plug in. If you have a mutual fund company with which you have all or most of your retirement money, that company's website will almost certainly have a retirement section where you can plug in your actual holdings and run alternatives for your retirement income plans.

Order of Withdrawal

You can increase the value of your retirement income by withdrawing from your various accounts in the proper order. First, if you are 70 ½ years of age or older, you may have to take regular minimum required distributions from your accounts. The amount you have to withdraw depends on your age, the age of your spouse and the balance in your account. The Internal Revenue Service issues a chart showing how to calculate the amount you must withdraw, and your broker, tax accountant or financial planner can help you know exactly how much you must take out. The required minimum distribution regulations apply to most employer sponsored accounts and to traditional individual retirement accounts. They do not apply to Roth IRAs because the main characteristic of the Roth is that you never have to withdraw funds unless you want to, and you do not pay income taxes on the withdrawals when you do.

As a side note, I would recommend you urge your children and others you care about to invest in a Roth IRA if they qualify and can possibly afford to do so. There is no investment better than the one on which you never have to pay taxes. I know some people worry that the government will renege on its promise, but erratic as our politicians are, they have a pretty good record of not changing tax laws retroactively. They might repeal the tax exemption for future contributions, but the money in the account should be safe. I am doubtful that even that is going to happen.

Second, if you need money beyond your required minimum distributions, you should look next to our investments that are outside any retirement accounts. In particular, you should look to those investments in which you have a high cost basis that will minimize your tax liabilities. For example, if you own 1000 shares of the JKL Company that you bought for $35 a share and another 1000 shares that you bought for $45 a share, you should sell the latter shares first. Since you paid more for the shares, you will have less profit, and therefore less capital gains taxes on your sale. This can get tricky, so you want to work closely with your broker on the transaction to be sure you are in compliance with regulations.

Third, you may have retirement accounts where all, or part, of your contributions were not tax deductible when you made them because your income was too high. For example, I have a traditional IRA that has some before-tax and some after-tax money in it. This is because when I made the contributions to the account, my income was too high to allow me to deduct the entire amount. It was low enough, however, that I could deduct a portion of the contribution. If you have an account of this type, you have probably filed IRS Form 8606 to record just how much of the balance of the account is in each category. This is the account you should withdraw from next because at least part of the money has already had the taxes paid. You want to postpone as long as possible taking money from accounts where you will have to pay taxes on all the money withdrawn.

Fourth, you can take money from your traditional qualified retirement plans on which you will have to pay taxes. That is because the dollars you and your employer put into the account were before-tax dollars. You did not pay taxes when the money went in, and you did not pay taxes on the earnings that accumulated through the years. So when the time comes to withdraw money during retirement, you will then face the tax liability.

Finally, if you still need more money after the above withdrawals, you can reach inside your Roth IRA. Because your Roth was funded with after–tax dollars, you will have no taxes to pay when these dollars are withdrawn. I believe your Roth account should be the last place you go for retirement money because these are funds that can continue to grow tax-free as long as you leave them in the account. If you are concerned about leaving a legacy, a good goal is to think about leaving all or a portion of your Roth for your spouse or heirs.

Your Other Investments

If you have an interest in investing, you probably have a diversified portfolio of other investments in addition to your retirement accounts. If you have plenty of income from your retirement and other accounts to meet your income needs in retirement, you may not need to change your investment strategy very much when you retire. If you do need to rely on your investments for income, you should consider adjusting your portfolio so that includes a good representation of stocks that have a history of paying dividends and regularly raising them. I did this with my portfolio as I approached retirement. I looked for companies that had paid a dividend for years, had stable and growing earnings that assured their ability to cover the dividend payments, and had a policy of regularly increasing those dividends. When I retired that list included stocks like Abbott Labs, Coca Cola, Colgate, Exxon, Pepsico and Pfizer. Utilities and preferred stocks are also good candidates for such a list.

Annuities

One of the areas of finance where there has been dramatic change in recent years is annuities. An annuity is a financial product that guarantees you an income for a specific period of time, often for your lifetime. Ten years ago I would have been very skeptical about anything I said concerning annuities because so many of them were flawed products. They often came with very high sales commissions up front for the person selling the annuity (often hidden) and high penalties if the buyer wanted to get out of the annuity in the first few years of ownership. They often included a set of "bells and whistles" that appeared to offer benefits that were often not delivered.

Much has changed in recent years. Regulation, self-regulation and competition have provided much improved annuity products. This is still a "buyer beware" area, but by doing some due diligence and comparative shopping, you should be able to find a product that meets your needs.

Who needs an annuity? I think retirees need a guaranteed, stable income that they can count on being there for their entire lives. Social Security is an example of an annuity that is guaranteed for life. It has the additional advantage of having cost-of-living adjustments. If you have a military pension or a retirement from a position as teacher, policeman, fireman, etc., you have an annuity-type income flow. Until about the 1980s many companies offered annuity-type retirement programs. More recently, an increasing number of retirement plans are based on

401k, 403b or similar programs. This means they do not necessarily guarantee a specific income level, nor do they give you an income for life. It is also likely the income flow will vary from year to year.

If most of your retirement income will come from Social Security and annuity-type pension programs, you may have no need to have an annuity. If most of your retirement income will come from qualified retirement plans, IRAs or your personal investments, you may want to take some of your balance and buy a guaranteed lifetime annuity. How much of your investments you want to place in an annuity depends on your risk tolerance and how much time and effort you want to devote to your investments in retirement.

Fortunately, this is an area where you can do comparative shopping. Many insurance and mutual fund companies offer annuity products. A good place to start your research would be at immediateannuities.com. This website allows you to input your age, amount of money you want to invest and other information, and it then projects what your annual annuity income will be. Our newsletter also shows annuity income projections each month. For example, at the beginning of 2012, $100,000 invested in an annuity would bring a 60 year old male a lifetime monthly income of $542. It would provide a 60 year old female a monthly payment of $501. If you wait until age 70 to buy the annuity, it will provide a male $680 monthly or a female $612 monthly for life.

Annuity payouts are based to some extent on interest rates at the time the annuity is purchased. The years 2011 and 2012 were times when interest rates were quite low. The payouts indicated above would have been higher had the interest rate environment been higher when the annuities were created. Once the annuity payouts are set, they remain the same for life unless you have some kind of cost of living or other adjustment as part of your annuity (for which you have paid a premium if you do). One way to protect yourself to some degree would be to stagger an annuity purchase. If you have $100,000 to invest, you could invest $50,000 now and a similar amount a year from now. That way if interest rates go up, your second annuity might pay a little more than the first one. Of course, interest rates could go the other direction. There are no guarantees.

Many university foundations, churches and other charitable organizations offer annuities that provide tax benefits. For example, you give an amount of money to your alma mater in return for which they provide you a life annuity. A portion of the money you give them is considered to be a gift and will qualify as a deduction on your income taxes. You should consult a tax advisor if you want to secure an annuity in this way.

There are many features that can be added to an annuity. You can provide for it to cover both you and your spouse. You can add a feature that provides a payout to beneficiaries for a given number of years even if you do not live long after securing the annuity. You can add a cost of living adjustment, although this is an expensive benefit. The more additional features you add to an annuity, the lower will be the monthly income that a given amount of money will buy.

Facing the Future

I remember, a number of years ago, when the young people who worked at McDonald's or other fast food places would look at me hesitantly, not sure whether to offer me the "senior discount" for fear that I would be offended. I learned to say "senior discount please" so as to take care of the uncertainty. Then it was not long before the hesitancy disappeared. They seemed quite sure I qualified and offered me the discount without question.

All of us face those events that remind us that we are getting older, and we need to recognize the consequences of that fact. It is a time when we give more attention to deciding how we will use our financial assets to help our loved ones and perhaps also our favorite philanthropic institutions—our university, church, synagogue, the Salvation Army, Red Cross or whatever your special interests might be. Then we must face the inevitable and devote some time to deciding how our resources will be managed and distributed after we are gone.

Helping Our Loved Ones

As we become senior citizens, I believe our first obligation to our children is to be sure they do not have to support us in our retirement years. That is why I believe that parents who are saving for the children's college educations should not give up funding their retirement accounts in order to do so. If they must, they might reduce their retirement contributions, but they should make at least some contributions there, even during their children's college years, because those retirement dollars will continue to grow tax-free or tax-deferred through the years. Working couples today often find themselves in a "sandwich" situation, trying to support their own families while also feeling pressure to help Mom and Dad. The best gift we can give our children is the assurance that we have provided for our own financial needs in our senior years.

Beyond providing for ourselves, I recognize that individuals have different opinions about how best to help our children and other loved ones. There is a point of view that says the best thing we can do for our children is to force them to be self-reliant, to "make it on their own." This is consistent with the point of view of those who want very high, almost confiscatory, estate taxes. They believe the government should decide where the great majority our financial resources go at the time of our death rather than letting us make that decision. I respect that view, but I disagree with it. My disagreement is a matter of degree. I am not in favor of completely repealing the estate tax, or what some prefer to call the death tax. I just believe it should be much lower than it is. If I were making the policy, I would make the first $10 million (inflation adjusted annually) of an estate completely exempt and have a tax of no more than 30% on the rest until you get to some very high figure, perhaps $100 million, at which a higher rate might be appropriate.

For many people, including me, one of the incentives for working hard and trying to build a reasonable level of wealth is so we can help our loved ones and those charitable institutions we want to support. My wife and I, like many others, also want to do what we can to help them while we are alive and can see the results of our help. Whether we are talking about our children or our charities, we also want to see how they use the help we are providing. If we like what we see, we can provide additional support. If not, we can make that known also.

Assuming you want to help your children or others, there are many ways to do so. Current federal tax law allows you to give up to $13,000 annually to each of your children (or anyone else, for that matter) with no tax implications at all. There is no tax liability to you or to the recipient of the gift. If you and your spouse both want to give, you can provide each recipient with $26,000. For most of us, this provision enables us to give away all we can afford to each year. For those of you who are able to give more, you can do so without creating a tax obligation by using your uniform credit which provides you an exemption from both gift and estate taxes. If you want to do this, you should talk to your tax advisor.

You can also help others by paying their medical or education expenses. When you do this you must make the payments directly to the medical or educational institution. The dollars must not pass through the hands of the beneficiary.

There are many other ways to help. If you own a business, you can provide part-time jobs for children or grandchildren in high school or college. I have a friend whose children are in their early working years. They are employed and have reasonable salaries but not enough to put away large amounts in savings. He has told them he would fund their IRAs for them, but he also warned them that the first time they withdraw any money to use on current expenses, that will be the last time he provides funds for the IRA. That seems like a reasonable financial arrangement to me.

Helping Others

One of the joys of achieving some level of wealth during your working years is the opportunity to use it to support causes and institutions that are important to you. Fortunately, federal tax law provides you incentives to make such contributions. As with gifts to your loved ones, straightforward cash gifts to charitable organizations are easy to make and should cause no tax problems. In fact, you can claim a tax deduction for your contributions in most cases so long as the contributions constitute less than 50% of your total adjusted gross income. Most of us cannot afford to give away half of our income, so this limit is not be a problem most of the time.

Subject to certain limits you can also give away items such as clothing, household goods, common stocks, bonds, real property, etc. If you bought shares of XYZ Company at $10 a share, and the price is now $20, you can give the stock to a charity and deduct it at the higher price. This is called a gift of "appreciated stock." You can also deduct unreimbursed expenses you incur while doing work for a charitable organization. For example, if you drive a car or ride a bus to a homeless shelter where you volunteer to work, you can deduct those expenses.

I would offer two words of advice. First, seek help from a tax professional if your contributions are in any way out of the ordinary. Second, do not let tax law drive your charitable activity. You support your church, university or other cause because you believe in them and want to help them achieve their goals, not primarily to get a tax break.

It would be presumptuous of me to try to tell others whether or how to give to worthwhile causes. That has to be a personal and/or family decision. In our family we try to choose a few causes that are of special concern to us. We give small amounts to quite a few organizations, but we try to choose a few causes in which we have a special interest and where we hope we can make some difference. You can decide what is of special interest to you. If you are giving to your university, you can choose to concentrate on student scholarships, the library or perhaps the department from which you graduated. If you want to make special contributions to your church or synagogue, you can direct them toward the youth program, music program or perhaps activities for seniors. A lifetime of investing is interesting, often fun, and hopefully profitable in the long run. For most of us, the opportunity to help our loved ones and support causes we believe in helps give meaning to our years of investing.

Estate Planning: "People Change. . ."

Through the years I have spoken at a number of investment seminars and conferences around the country. Another person who often speaks at the same meetings is a specialist in estate planning from Florida named Dr. Joe Gandolfo. Joe has an impressive deep resonant voice. He often begins his lecture by proclaiming in a booming voice, "People change when people die!" For emphasis, he sometimes repeats, "People change when people die!" He is making a very valid point.

My own experience tells how true his statement is. Family members who all seem to get along beautifully, enjoy family reunions and visit regularly often change dramatically when a senior family member passes away. Questions of "who gets what?" or "who decides who gets what?" become all-important and break families apart. Often little things take on great meaning.

How the bank account or the stock portfolio is divided is crucial, but questions of who gets Dad's coin collection or who gets Grandma's pearl necklace, that she inherited from her grandma can be just as instrumental in aggravating family feuds or personal resentment. Joe is right. People change.

I have no expertise to tell people how to do their estate planning. I have just one recommendation: *find the best estate planning attorney you can find.* Ask your friends who they recommend. Ask your attorney, broker or financial planner the same question. Look for an attorney for whom estate planning is a specialty, not a sideline. On Saturday mornings I sometimes listen to a radio talk show hosted by a household do-it-yourself expert. If you have a question about remodeling your bathroom or fixing the leak in the roof, he is he person to ask. He can tell you what to do and whether to get your supplies at Lowe's, Home Depot or Wal-Mart. He is a do-it-yourself advocate, but he also tells us something very important. He reminds us that the two most important tools in our toolbox are a cell phone and a checkbook. He is saying that, even for the ardent do-it-yourself person, there are times when we need to call the expert and pay them to do the job for us.

I have advocated a do-it-yourself approach through most of this book. Sixty years in the stock market have convinced me that individual investors, if they so choose and are willing to make the effort, can do much of the asset allocation, security selection, portfolio management, rebalancing and related activities themselves. The time comes, however, when the best thing to do is to call the expert. I believe estate planning is one of those times. Before you see an attorney, there are some things you can do to make your work with your estate attorney more effective.

Perhaps the first point to note is that estate planning should not be put off until your retirement years. A young couple will need documents that describe who is to take care of their children in case of their own death or disability.. An individual who is responsible for the care of a child or sibling with disabilities should have legal papers that describe what should happen in case that individual can no longer meet their responsibilities.

When you visit your attorney, you should have a general idea of what you want him to do. In most cases your estate planning documents should include:

(1) Will
(2) Trust documents (as needed)
(3) Living will
(4) Medical power of attorney
(5) Durable power of attorney (for financial, property and non-medical matters)

One decision you will need to make before you visit your attorney is who you want to be in charge of your assets after your death. This person may be called an "executor," "administrator," "personal representative" or some other term depending on the state where you live. You need to give some thought to this. You may choose a close friend, a business associate, an accountant or attorney, or you may choose a family member. If you choose a family member, it is wise to make it clear to other family members why you chose the person you did. For example, you may choose your oldest child or the one who is an attorney or financial professional. Other family members may not agree with your decision, but they will understand it.

After your legal documents are completed, you will want to be sure that someone other

than you and your spouse know where they are. The days of having just one set of documents locked away in a safe deposit box are over. In the day of the copy machine it is easy for you to provide copies of various documents to whomever you think should have them. For example, you will probably want your primary care physician to have a copy of your living will and medical power of attorney.

One responsibility that is primarily yours rather than your attorney's is to specify the beneficiary on bank accounts, certificates of deposit, insurance policies, retirement accounts, etc. This has the practical effect of enabling the designated beneficiary to receive the proceeds of those accounts quickly and without going through probate or other legal process.

Finally, it is important to keep your documents up to date. Legal documents that state your wishes at age 65 might not reflect your preferences at age 80 or 85. Deaths, marriages, changing needs of family members, sudden increased health costs and similar unexpected events can cause your estate planning goals to change. You will want to meet with your attorney from time to time, perhaps every five years, to be sure your documents state your current preferences and goals.

Summing Up

I will conclude by noting, as I have throughout the pages of the book, that one of the most important lessons I have learned over sixty years is that there is no "holy grail" in the world of investing. There is no secret formula or strategy that allows a few privileged people, perhaps hedge fund managers or those with a Ph.D. in mathematics from M.I.T., to accumulate great wealth while the rest of us are denied the same opportunity. The collapse of Long Term Capital Management and Lehman Brothers, both run by people we thought were the best in the business, illustrate that point well. Rather, the best investment strategies are among those that are the easiest to understand and the simplest to implement. I am thinking of strategies such as asset allocation, the advantageous use of time, careful attention to expenses, protecting your existing resources and using index funds.

Asset allocation is always the single most important investment strategy. It reduces risk and provides exposure to the various classes of investments that provide profit opportunities. I am not a fanatic on this. I don't believe one can be so precise as to know that a portfolio should be exactly 53.5% in stocks, 26.9% in bonds, etc. The individual investor, however, can make intelligent decisions that set his allocations at 60% stocks, 30% bonds or whatever they prefer. An advantage of asset allocation is that it enables an investor to adjust a portfolio to allow for his own level of risk tolerance.

We use asset allocation because of another lesson I have learned over sixty years: no one can predict the future direction of the stock market. We need to be wary of those who tell us they can. Those who spend a lot of time studying their investments and the stock market in general can use their research time in two ways. They can spend time trying to figure out how to predict the market, or they can devote their time to trying to discover strategies that will provide a reasonable investment return over the years without having to predict the market. They are much better off following the latter course.

The fact that even the best of us, including mutual fund managers and securities analysts, cannot predict the market is one reason I am a strong advocate of index funds. I enjoy active investing. I try to pick individual stocks that will do well, and I feel good when I can "beat the market." I feel more confident with my active investing, however, because I know I have a solid base of index funds providing a strong foundation under my investments.

Index funds illustrate another fundamental truth about investing, which is that high expenses equal reduced profits. When index funds outperform actively managed funds, as they often do, it is not because the managers of active funds are less competent or uninformed. They just have to deal with the higher expenses that are a natural part of their work environment. They have to work harder to make up for the fact their fund returns are being compared to index funds and benchmarks that do not face the same expenses they do. The problem of excessively high expenses applies not just to mutual funds but to all aspects of investing. The individual investor needs to constantly seek low brokerage fees, minimal portfolio turnover, tax deferral or tax exemption (Roth) whenever possible. The extent to which investors can control expenses like these will have a direct impact on their investment success.

One lesson investors learn quickly—you don't need sixty years—is that there is no substitute for doing your homework. It takes a lot of preparation to be a good long distance runner or weight lifter, and the same is true of investors. Hard work, discipline and research are prerequisites for successful investing.

Fortunately, individual investors today have a wealth of tools and research sources to rely on. Good websites, financial news, magazines and television sources are all available, some at little or no cost. With modest but consistent effort, the individual investor today can be an informed investor.

Finally, a crucial lesson to remember is that investing is not the primary purpose of life. It is a means to an end. Our families, faith, values, service to others and our commitment to making the world of our grandchildren better than the world of today are things that really matter. Successful investing can help make that happen.

Chapter 11
Random Thoughts

The articles in this chapter have all appeared in *No-Load Portfolios* in recent years. Bill Corney and I work on most of the newsletter jointly. The only portion of the newsletter which represents the personal opinion of one of us is the page 3 article entitled "Commentary." We alternate, with Bill writing the article one month and me writing it the next. The articles published here are ones that I have written, and represent my opinions only.

What Has Changed in 25 Years?
Published January, 2010

As we begin our 25th year of publishing this newsletter, it is mind-boggling to think about the things that have changed in that time. The Dow Jones Industrial Average was at 1211.57 on January 1, 1985. Since that time we have seen the market collapse of October, 1987, the bull market of the 1990s and the bursting of three bubbles—savings and loan in the 1980s, technology "dot.com" in 2000 and real estate in 2008-09. Today interest rates are near zero, while 25 years ago Fed Chair Paul Volcker has pushed rates to unprecedented levels attempting to break the back of inflation. Treasury bill rates were near 20%, and I briefly had a 13 5/8% mortgage.

There are a variety of investment products that were not available then. The idea of an investment that would "guarantee" to stay ahead of inflation was unknown. Today we have Treasury inflation-protected securities that can be bought directly from the Treasury or through buying a mutual fund or ETF. It was difficult in 1985 for the individual investor to add real estate, precious metals or commodities to a portfolio. Today ETFs make it possible to own agricultural or natural resource commodities, gold, silver, coal, timber, etc. to fill a specific niche in a portfolio. The computer and internet have empowered individual investors so that they can make use of information and analytical tools once available only to investment professionals and large firms.

Some things have not changed as much. Asset allocation is still one of the most effective strategies for managing portfolio risk, and the new ETFs mentioned above make it possible to be very precise in adding to specific asset categories.. Long-term investing, rather than quick in-and-out trading, is still the best approach for the individual investor. Minimizing investment expenses through use of index funds, using a discount or internet broker, buying no-load mutual funds, minimizing portfolio turnover and reading *No-Load Portfolios* were good strategies in 1985, and they still are.

Some of our favorite analysts like John Templeton and Louis Rukeyser are gone. We still have the opportunity to learn from great minds like John Bogle, Warren Buffett, Robert Shiller, Bill Gross and others. In the future we will learn from new, young voices we do not yet know. We expect the next 25 years to be at least as exciting as the past.

The Bernie Madoff Saga: Relearning What We Already Knew
Published June, 2009

The story of Bernie Madoff's $13 billion ponzi scheme is a tragedy of epic proportions. Thousands of individuals were left financially destitute and families saw a lifetime of savings disappear in an instant. The fact that he is sentenced to 150 years in prison may provide some satisfaction, but the likelihood is that most of the losses are gone forever. Another sad fact is that, when we examine the story closely, we don't learn very much new about financial matters. The story simply confirms what we already know. For example consider the following.

If it sounds too good to be true, it probably is. If someone offers you a financial product that pays you 10%-12% a year consistently, in good times and bad with little variation, it is time to be skeptical. Investments fluctuate in price, and the higher the return, the more risk is attached to them. This leads to the next obvious point.

If you don't understand it, don't invest in it. Another way of saying this is, "Investigate before you invest." Too often I have had people say, "I'm not sure just what this is; it's an annuity or a kind of insurance policy or something." You don't have to be a broker or a corporate lawyer, but you should learn the basic differences between bonds, stocks, mutual funds, certificates of deposit, etc. and the varying risks involved in each. Know what you are investing in.

Don't let personal loyalties overrule common sense. I have known people reluctant to change their doctor, dentist, attorney, broker or financial advisor because they didn't want to offend them or because they are a personal friend. Don't get caught in that trap. If you need to make a change, work up the courage and do what you know needs to be done.

Once again—diversify, diversify, diversify! We say it over and over because it is so fundamental to good investment practice. There is no investment in the world so good that it deserves to have all of your money invested in it. If you think you have discovered the perfect investment, study it and understand what it is. Then put perhaps 10% of your funds into it. Watch it over time, and if it does well, add more to it gradually. You won't get rich over night that way, but you may avoid a lot of severe financial pain.

The Explosion in Exchange-Traded Funds
Published May, 2011

Morningstar recently reported that the total value of exchange-traded funds in circulation has passed the $1.0 trillion mark. ETFs are portfolios of securities that resemble mutual funds in many ways but also have important differences. A significant difference is that ETFs trade on an exchange and, unlike mutual funds, they trade and fluctuate in value throughout the time the market is open. Mutual funds are valued only once each day; the do not fluctuate in price throughout the day. ETFs usually have very low annual expense ratios, a major advantage for the individual investor.

The oldest of these funds have been around less than 20 years. The first was an S&P500 fund established in 1993 and many ETFs today are still based on some index. Some of our readers have questioned why we write about these funds in our newsletter since they are not literally "no-load" funds. We like them, however, because the annual expenses are so low and trading costs can be low as well. Some companies such as Fidelity and Schwab have their own ETFs that they will sell to clients at no cost, making them "no load" funds in that case.

ETFs have many advantages. For example, if you want to build a simple index portfolio including large-cap, mid-cap, small-cap, bond and inflation-linked bond funds, you can easily do with ETFs. You can then rebalance annually with minimal transaction costs (no costs if you work within one firm that offers its funds at no fee). I have a basic portfolio of exactly this type that I maintain at a discount broker. I make few changes in it, mainly annual rebalancing, and those transactions, made through my computer, cost only a few dollars each.

If you have a more complex portfolio, ETFs can be used to fill in those specific areas you want to include. For example, if you want to include the BRIC countries—Brazil, Russia, India and China—in your portfolio, you can buy an ETF that invests just in those markets, iShares MSCI BRIC (BRK). There are also funds for each country, for example iShares MSCI Brazil Index (EWZ). You can be a specific as looking for a small cap fund, Market Vectors Brazil Small Cap (BRF). ETFs give you the ability to fill a specific niche in your portfolio.

Many investors are now wanting to add commodities to their holdings, and ETFs are an ideal way to do so. Whether you want to add energy, precious metals, financial or agricultural holdings, there are funds to meet that need. Powershares DB Commodity Index (DBC) is a comprehensive fund that holds many different types of commodities. Our February Tip of the Month discussed the Market Vectors Agribusiness ETF (MOO), a fund for those who want to include agriculture in their diversified portfolio.

An All-Bond Portfolio
Published July, 2010

As a financial planner, I recently had an individual ask me if it would be possible for him to have a portfolio avoiding stocks and owning only bond and money market mutual funds. I told him I believed most investors' portfolios should include stocks most of the time, but that there will be those who prefer not to own stocks. They may simply believe the risk of falling stock prices exceeds the risk of rising interest rates, which will cause bonds to lose value. They may also want to avoid stocks for a specific period of time, patiently waiting for equity conditions to improve. Those in and near retirement may also choose to have little or no exposure to stocks.

After a lengthy discussion, I told him that if he wanted a portfolio including no stocks and using only bond mutual funds, I would recommend one for him. Because he was familiar with Vanguard mutual funds and had a brokerage account there, I based my recommendations on their funds. One could develop a similar portfolio with the funds of Fidelity, T. Rowe Price and other no-load fund firms. One should also consider using the funds shown in our Income Portfolio on page 2. The Vanguard portfolio I recommended to him is as follows:

Intermediate Term Bond Fund (BVIIX)	40%
GNMA Fund (VFIIX)	15%
Corporate High Yield Fund (VWEHX)	10%
Intermediate Term Investment Grade Fund (VFICX)	15%
Inflation Protected Bond Fund (VIPSX)	10%
Prime Money Market Fund (VMMXX)	10%

I have included no long term funds to reduce the potential loss when interest rates start to rise, which they will at some point. Long term bond funds will get hurt the most. For a nimble investor, I would have no objection to starting with some investment in thc Long Term Bond fund and using the Short Term Bond fund in place of the Money Market fund since it is paying essentially 0%. When interest rates start to rise, the Long Term fund could be sold with the proceeds going to the Intermediate Term fund and the Inflation Protected Bond fund. The Short Term bond fund could also be sold with the proceeds moved to the Money Market fund.

One could add other asset categories to a portfolio, while still avoiding stocks, by including precious metals, commodities, currencies, real estate investment trusts, etc. If one specifically wants an all bond portfolio, however, consider something like the one shown here.

A Portfolio for Those Wary of Stocks
Published September, 2010

In the July newsletter I discussed an all-bond portfolio that I had developed for an individual who had become wary of stocks. While I pointed out that I believe a good asset allocation should include stocks, I also recognized that one can build a good portfolio without stocks if preferred. The July portfolio included only bonds of various duration and type, but there are other asset categories that can provide return and help limit risk in a portfolio. Note that some of the funds discussed below own stocks, but the asset categories are such that they should reduce overall risk because their price movements are not directly correlated with major stock indexes.

Precious metals. Many investors want to own at least some precious metals as a hedge against inflation or the loss of valuation of the dollar against other currencies. The largest exchange-traded fund here is *SPDR Gold Shares* (GLD), providing direct ownership of gold bullion. Silver is another precious metal alternative (see the Odds & Ends section for more information). Three mutual funds worth considering are *Fidelity Select Gold* (FSAGX), *American Century Global Gold* (BGEIX), and *Vanguard Precious Metals and Mining* (VGPMX).

Commodities. If you would like to add commodities as an asset category, there are two comprehensive ETFs that include most of the various commodity sectors: *PowerShares DB Commodity Index (DBC) and Dow Jones AIG Commodity Index Total Return (DJP).* A good traditional mutual fund is T. Rowe Price New Era (PRNEX), which tends to emphasize the energy sector. If you prefer a specific commodity area there are funds you can select in agriculture (MOO), coal (KOL), lumber (CUT), oil (USO), natural gas (FGC), water (FTW), etc.

Real estate. There are numerous REITs and real estate funds to choose from. A broad based ETF is *iShares Dow Jones Real Estate* (IYR). Good funds include *Fidelity Real Estate* (FRESX), *T. Rowe Price Real Estate* (TRREX) *and Vanguard REIT*, which can be owned as an ETF (VNQ) or a mutual fund (VGSIX).

A total portfolio. Putting it together, a portfolio might include 60% bonds, 15% real estate, 15% commodities and 10% precious metals. You can adjust the numbers to meet your goals and risk tolerance, but bonds should be the major holding in a portfolio of this type.

The World's Greatest Financial Newsletter
Published March, 2010

No, I am not talking about *No-Load Portfolios,* although I would be glad if I could proclaim it the world's greatest. I am talking about a newsletter mentioned in an article by Mark Hulbert, publisher of *Hulbert's Financial Digest* and the person who knows more about financial newsletters than anyone else I know.

Mark's newsletter has often given *NLP* very high ratings and we appreciate that. In the February, 2010 edition of his publication he has an article about a newsletter named *Closed-End Country Fund Report.* Among all the newsletters Hulbert monitors, this one ranked in first place for portfolio performance over the last five and ten year periods. The amazing thing about this story, however, is that this newsletter has not published a new edition since 2004! Since the newsletter has never officially announced it was ceasing publication, Hulbert continues to monitor its portfolio assuming it has made no changes since that October, 2004 edition.

Is this just a strange anomaly or is there something to be learned from this situation? Obviously, no one would be likely to recommend going the past six years without one change in a portfolio. That would be the ultimate buy and hold strategy. However, the story does affirm some things we already knew about investing. First, it reminds us that long-term investing is usually more successful than short-term investing. Second, a related point is that high portfolio turnover has a negative impact on investment return. A high level of buying and selling in our portfolio causes us to do less weall with out investing. Turnover causes two expenses, brokerage transaction costs and taxes. John Bogle estimates that 100% turnover increases costs by about one per cent. A portfolio with 50% annual turnover will raise transactions costs about 0.5%.

Because of the experience with the *Closed-End* newsletter, Hulbert compared the 2009 returns of all the portfolios he follows with what the returns would have been had no changes been made in the portfolios during the entire year. The average annual return of the portfolios for the year was 28.7%. Assuming they made no changes throughout the year and just stuck with their beginning of the year recommendations, the average return would have been 29.4%, or 0.7% better than the actual returns that included all the recommended changes during the year.

If you follow our page 2 portfolios you know we make few changes over a year's time. We agree with Hulbert, Bogle and other students of investing that long-term investment horizons and low portfolio turnover are two important steps toward successful and profitable investing.

Asset Allocation –The Details
Published June, 2009

I have often written about the importance of asset allocation as a fundamental first step in developing an investment strategy. There is plenty of research that shows that asset allocation strategy is the single most important factor in determining long-term investment returns. I have perhaps been remiss, however, in not writing more about the details of what an asset allocation plan should look like. Historically, plans have included three categories: (1) equities (stocks), (2) fixed income securities and (3) cash and cash equivalents. In more recent years many investors have added two new categories: (4) real estate and (5) precious metals. It would be quite appropriate for a small investor to choose just one mutual fund for each of the categories. As one's portfolio grows, however, it makes sense to diversify within each category, as follows.

Stocks. If you have room for two stocks or funds in this category, you should include both large-cap and small-cap investments. You should also have international investments here, such as those on page 6. You can also divide your holdings into "value" and "growth."

Fixed income. You can use just one general bond fund here. Alternatively, you can own short-term, intermediate-term and long-term bond funds. If you are in a high income bracket, you might want to invest mainly in tax-free municipal bonds or funds. You can also include inflation-protected bonds and international funds.

Real estate. You can diversify this category by owning RE-ITs or funds that hold residential property, commercial property, industrial property, overseas property, etc. You might also include funds that hold mortgages, construction companies, remodeling companies, etc.

Precious metals. You can invest in funds that own the metals directly, but you can also own funds that hold mines, processing companies, etc. You can also hold funds that own different metals—gold, silver, platinum, etc.

Cash. You can hold your cash in money market funds, CDs, savings accounts, Treasury bills, etc. Finally, as I noted in this column in July, you might want to add a new category to your asset allocation plan, commodities.

The Active vs. Passive Management Debate: Revisited One More Time
Published September, 2009

The stock market volatility of the last eighteen months has generated renewed interest in the debate about active versus passive management of portfolios. For more than half a century, going back at least to the Modern Portfolio Theory literature of the 1950s, investors have asked whether active management can really beat just investing in a portfolio of good index funds. The active management activists argue that by picking good stocks, avoiding bad ones and moving into cash when the market turns down that they can outperform passive investing in index funds. Passive advocates say that investing is a zero sum game, the losers will always equal the winners, and no one can know ahead of time which will be which. They also argue that because index funds have much lower annual expenses than actively managed funds, they will provide superior long-term returns. The active management argument is well stated in two recent books: Ken Solow's *Buy and Hold is Dead (Again)* and *The Myth of the Rational Market,* by Justin Fox. The passive, or index fund, argument is presented persuasively in *The Smartest Investment Book You'll Ever Read,* by Daniel Solin, and *The Little Book of Common Sense Investing,* by John Bogle.

My analysis of the research through the years says that the index fund argument makes a good case. A Standard and Poor's study of the five years ending June 30 found that only 37.1% of the actively managed large-cap funds beat the S&P500 over that period, 26.6% of mid-cap fund managers beat the S&P 400 and 42.6% of small-cap funds beat the benchmark S&P600. The books mentioned give you much more information to help you make up your own mind.

Regular readers know that this newsletter recommends both actively managed and index funds. I would recommend that most investors have a foundation portfolio of index funds which they hold for the long term, and then add actively managed funds on top of that, carefully selecting funds that meet specific goals such as income, capital appreciation or asset allocation. In the Odds and Ends section of this newsletter we present the argument for why active investing may be preferable in the current investment environment. In buying either actively or passively managed funds, remember the characteristics that make both kinds profitable—no loads, low annual expenses, low turnover, good asset allocation and strict avoidance of the manager who says he can consistently "time the market" and "find the next big unidentified stock winner" to make you rich almost overnight.

Rebalancing: An Essential Step In Asset Allocation
Published November, 2010

This is the time of year when investors begin to think about rebalancing their portfolios. Rebalancing is the process of bringing your portfolio back into line with your desired asset allocation goals. For example, if you want to have an allocation of 60% stocks and 40% bonds, and a rising market has taken your stocks to where they constitute 68% of your portfolio, you will want to take steps to move back toward the 60/40 goal.

If you are fortunate to have investment money available, you can rebalance by adding to your bond holdings. If you don't have money available, you can rebalance by selling some of your stocks and using the money to buy bonds or bond funds. This gives you a chance to decide what stocks or stock funds to sell. You may have some "losers" you are glad to get rid of. As an alternative, you may want to take profits from some of your stocks that have done well. I don't like to have any one stock or stock fund constitute more than 10% of my portfolio. Therefore, if stocks have risen sharply, I may sell some to raise funds for rebalancing and also to bring it back within my 10% limit.

When to rebalance. I usually rebalance toward the end of the year, but if it is better for your schedule to do so in mid-summer, spring or some other time, that will work also. I do it around year end to take advantage of the tax laws. If I need to sell a stock or fund that involves a capital gain, I want to do it in January so that I can postpone my capital gains tax payment until April of the following year. If I am taking a capital loss, I try to do so in December, so I can take advantage of the loss on my current year tax return.

How often to rebalance. I rebalance annually, and most research shows there is little to be gained by doing so more often.

Some do it semi-annually or even quarterly, and there is nothing wrong with that so long as you stick to it. The danger is that the more often you decide to rebalance, the less likely you are to stick with it and actually do it. Some rebalance whenever their portfolio gets more than 5% out of balance. For example, if their goal is to have 60% in stocks, they will rebalance when their stock holdings move above 65% or below 55%. How and when you rebalance is less important than that you have the self-discipline to do it. Asset allocation is essential to the goal of reducing risk in a portfolio, and rebalancing is an essential step in the asset allocation process.

Year-End Planning for Investors
Published November, 2011

As the end of the year approaches, it is a good time for investors to review their portfolios and prepare for 2012. There are several steps worth taking as we look ahead.

Rebalancing. Rebalancing is the process of bringing your portfolio back into line with your desired asset allocation goals. It should usually be done annually, but there are not always reasons that make it necessary to do it at the end of the year. If all of your rebalancing is done inside retirement and other tax-protected accounts, there are no tax implications in the process. However, if your rebalancing involves selling securities that have capital gains or losses, you can use the year-end calendar to your advantage. If you are selling stocks on which you have a capital gain, you should wait until January to do your selling. This pushes your gains into next year and postpones any tax liability by fifteen months, to April 15, 2013, when you have to file your 2012 tax return. If, on the other hand, you are selling stocks where you have a capital loss, you should sell before the end of the year. That way you can take the loss in the current year, when you file your 2011 tax return next April.

Reviewing goals. Changing circumstances can cause changes in goals. Marriage, divorce, birth of a child, job change, job loss or sending a child off to college can all be reasons to rethink your investment goals and perhaps your asset allocation targets. The beginning of a new year is a good time to think about whether there are changes in your situation that will impact on your investment strategies.

Portfolio clean-up. I sometimes find "dribs and drabs" in my portfolio that I would rather not have. A stock may have spun off a subsidiary, leaving me an odd number of shares of something I have never heard of. Or I may find that what I thought would be tomorrow's "hot stock" turned out instead to be today's "dud." There is almost always the opportunity to upgrade a portfolio, to weed out a few weak holdings and generally improve your investment experience. The beginning of a new year is a good time to do it.

CPSIA information can be obtained at www.ICGtesting.com
Printed in the USA
BVOW012003300512

291411BV00006B/6/P